The Obama Effect

~

The Rise of Trumpism
&
Christian Response

TONY L. SCOTT

Copyright © 2025 by Tony L. Scott. All rights reserved.
ISBN: 979-8-9929197-3-8 (Hard Cover)

No part of this book may be reproduced or used in any manner without written permission of the copyright owner, except for the use of quotations in a book review.

For more information or permissions, please contact the author:
redeemedwriter718@gmail.com
tlmdscott2@gmail.com

Editor: This book was self-edited by the author.

DEDICATION

To my grandson, Harrison, and his parents, Desmond and Lauren;
To my granddaughters, Rumi and Mina, and their parents, Mario and Negin;
And to my loving and selfless wife, Lisa. Thank you for being everything that I need.

May this work be a lamp to your feet and a light to your path. May you be rooted in truth, fortified in faith, and equipped to navigate the urgencies of these times. Let it serve not only as a guide for your journey but as a testament for generations yet unborn—a legacy of wisdom, discernment, and the enduring hope of God's kingdom.

Table of Contents

About the Author 1
Author's Note 3
Preface 5
Introduction 7

Chapter 1: The Machine of Empire: An Engine Against African Americans and Indigenous Progress 11
    The Cost of Empire: Native Lands and Mexican Loss 14
    The Early Bonds of the Oppressed 17
    Bacon's Rebellion and the Birth of Whiteness 19
    The Birth of Race Through Empire and Colonization 23
    Brutality and Dehumanization Tactics of Enslavers 25
    Systems and Systemic Machinery That Oppress Blacks 28
    Christian Response 30

Chapter 2: The Journey to Civil Rights, Yet the Struggle Continues 33
    The Cornerstone Speech and Confederate Ideologies 33
    The 13th, 14th, 15th Reconstruction Amendments 35
    The 24th and 26th Amendments 38
    Timeline: The Journey of Struggle and Resistance 39
    The Reconstruction Era: 1865–1877 41
    Jim Crow and the Legalization of Segregation 44
    The Great Migration: 1916–1970 45
    The Renaissance Period: Cultural and Intellectual Awakening 49
    White Backlash in the 20th Century 51
    Link to the Road to Civil Rights 52
    Faith as the Engine of Freedom 54
    The Civil Rights Legacy and Its Continuing Assault 54
    Christian Response 59

Chapter 3: Freedom Rising: Hope, Sacrifice, and The Blood of the Movement 63
    The Groveland Four, Emmett Till, and the Moral Spark of a Movement, 1949–1955 66
    The Little Rock Nine, Greensboro Sit-Ins, and Freedom Rides, 1957–1961 68
    The March on Washington, 16th Street Baptist Church Bombing, and Montgomery Marches, 1963–1965 69
    The Assassinations of Malcolm X, Dr. King, and Nationwide Riots, 1965–1968 71
    Dr. Martin Luther King and Malcolm X: Revered and Feared Targets of Racial Supremacy 72
    Christian Response 75

Chapter 4: Growing Up Black in America, The Weight and the Witness of Survival 77
    The Welfare State and the Wounding of the Black Family 79
    The Thirst that Could Not Be Quenched 81
    Playing While Black 83
    Experiences of Racism in Young Adulthood 85
    Christian Response 89

Chapter 5: The Trumps: Father, Son, and the Systems - A Legacy of American Racism 93
    Fred Trump: The Patriarch and the Pattern 93
    Donald Trump: The Inheritance of Racism 95
    The Intergenerational Logic of White Supremacy 98
    Redlining and Economic Oppression 99
    The Racial Wealth Gap and Housing Discrimination 102
    School-to-Prison Pipeline, Historical Roots, and Modern Realities 104
    Overcoming Racial Trauma Through Faith and Resilience 108
    Christian Response 110

Chapter 6: The Smoke Before the Fire: Rodney King and O.J. Simpson 113
    The Beating of Rodney King, 1991 — Violence Caught on Camera ... 116
    The 1992 Los Angeles Riots — Outrage Erupts 118
    Media Portrayal and the Machinery of Division 119
    White Alarm and Re-entrenchment: Fear Turns to Reaction 121
    Lasting Impact on Race Relations 123
    Christian Response 127

Chapter 7: God, Family, Country: The Rise of Christian Nationalism and the Politics of Fear 129
    Christian Nationalism Comes Out of the Shadows 129
    The Myth of a Christian Founding and the Golden Past 130
    Mainstreaming of White Grievance Through Churches...................... 130
    Early Alliances with Conservative Power Brokers 131
    Prophets of a New Dominion — The New Apostolic Reformation 131
    Conservative Media as Radicalization Engine — Fox News, Rush Limbaugh, and the Outrage Machine 132
    The Revival of White-Power Movements — Militias, Identity, and the Digital Turn 134
    The Moral and Practical Stakes... 137
    The Theology of Manifest Destiny, Reborn.. 137
    Christian Response 140

Chapter 8: The Great Replacement: Panic, Suppression, Revision, and the Struggle for Power 141
    Demographic Anxiety Becomes Crisis Rhetoric 141
    "We Are Losing Our Country" Becomes a Conservative Slogan 143
    Great Replacement Theory in U.S. Form 146
    Voter Suppression as Political Strategy.. 148
    Whitewashing the Past to Control the Present 150
    "Heritage Not Hate" — Patriotism as Cover for Oppression 152
    Conservative Media Finishes Mainstreaming Extremism 153
    Militia + Christian Nationalism Convergence..................................... 155

White Identity Becomes "Sacred Identity" 155
Defenders of "American Christianity" 156
Christian Response 158
The Kingdom Is Not America 159
The Call Forward 159

Chapter 9: The Obama Effect & The Counter-Revolution Against Hope 161

November 4, 2008. The Nation Held Its Breath 161
Hope and Shock: The First Black President — Global Celebration, Local Disbelief 163
White Political Identity Becomes Explicit: "Take Our Country Back" and the Tea Party 164
The Birth of Trumpism and the Birther Movement: Weaponizing a Name 165
Normalizing Racism in Mainstream Politics: From Dog Whistles to Bullhorns 165
Cultural Conflict Under Obama 167
The Fight Over Confederate Symbols Intensifies 167
Policy Battles Revealing Racial Lines 168
Resurgence of Efforts to Silence Black History and Erase Trauma 170
The Moral Compass of a Nation Fractured 171
Christian Response 174

Chapter 10: A Nation at the Breaking Point: Race, Justice, and The Battle for America's Soul 177

The Blood That Reopened America's Wound 177
A Country Confronts Its Reflection 179
Charleston: The Sanctuary Breached — June 17, 2015 180
The Rise of Modern Social Justice Movements 183
Black Lives Matter: What We Believe 186
What We Believe – Est. 7/13/13, Founders Alicia Garza, Patrisse Khan-Cullors, and Opal Tometi 187
Conservative Perception 190

    Why These Movements Triggered a Different Kind of Backlash 194
    The Fusion: "Trojan Horse" Narratives and Moral Panic 195
    The Coming Storm — A Population Believing Violence May Be
    Necessary 197
    Social Fracture Deepens: Racial Resentment, Distrust, Demonization . 199
    Reality: Two Threat Narratives, Two Survival Logics 200
    Christian Response 203

Chapter 11: The Trump Era of White Supremacy, 2016–2020 207
    Trump's Election and the Resurgence of Racism (2016) 207
    Immediate Societal Implications and Concerns within Black
    and Minority Communities 208
    Charlottesville and the Public Display of White Supremacy (2017) 209
    White Privilege, Immigration, and Policy Selectivity 210
    The Erasure of Black History in Education 212
    George Floyd's Murder and the 2020 Global Protests 213
    The Intersection of Justice and "Woke" Politics 214
    Christian Response 217

**Chapter 12: The Burden of Representation: Obama, Trump, Biden,
and Harris in a Divided America (2008–2024) 219**
    Barack Obama — The Promise and the Peril of a Black Presidency
    (2008–2016) 219
    Resistance in Real Time 221
    The Moral Paradox of Progress 224
    The Afterglow and the Undercurrent 226
    The Return of the Old Order: Trump and the Politics of Retaliation
    (2016–2020) 227
    Impeachments, Investigations, and the Absence of Accountability 230
    Joe Biden — Continuity, Crisis, and the Politics of Fatigue
    (2021–2024) 232
    The Battle for the Nation's Soul 233
    The Shadow of Trumpism 235

    Kamala Harris: Breaking Barriers and Bearing Burdens (2021–2024).. 236
    Continuity, Collapse, and the Lessons of Leadership 239
    The Prelude to Trump's Return 240
    Christian Response 242

Chapter 13: The Trumpian Ascendancy: Race, Power, and The New American Order 2025 → 245

    The Shock Before the Shift 245
    Orderly Transference and the Shadow of the Abuse of Power 247
    The Return of Trump and the Deepening Division 248
    Unmaking the Promises: Executive Power Rollbacks and the Rise of Trumpianism Redux 251
    Cultural and Historical Erasure: Reclaiming the Lost America 254
    Authoritarianism, Violence, and Political Suppression 256
    Gerrymandering and the New Architecture of Power 258
    The American Crisis and the New Global Order 260
    The Cause and The Continuum 262
    Christian Response 263

Chapter 14: The Future of America: Racial Justice and Its Uncertainty. 265

    How Did We Get Here? 265
    From Discovery to Domination — The American Continuum 266
    The Church at the Crossroads of History 267
    Where Do We Go from Here? 268
    Christian Response 271

Postscript 275

    The Burden and the Hope 275

About the Author

Minister Tony L. Scott, a U.S. Army Veteran, Retired Police Officer and a preacher, now over three decades, is the author of several works exploring faith, history, and human destiny, including ***The Cause of Empire:*** Colonization, Civilization, Extermination — The Echoes That Built Our World... ***Christianity: The White Man's Religion?*** — The Great Lie, Reclaiming Biblical Truth... ***A Comprehensive Study on the Book of Revelation;*** and ***A Family Journey Through the Bible***. His additional writings, including ***Not What I Wanted, Nevertheless, Everything That I Needed... Dad The Difference Maker, Dad The Dilemma,*** as well as ***Sentinel of Service, Protecting Durham, Protecting the Bull City*** — Policing's Evolution, Nationally and Locally, Preserving the Legacy of the Historic Hayti District, continue his mission to illuminate truth, reconcile history, and strengthen faith across generations.

Author's Note

As the author of this book, I write from a dual perspective. I stand both as a witness to the present and as a student of the past, fully aware that history is not static but living — breathing through every age and generation. Many of the pages that follow were written in real time, amidst the turbulence of a nation wrestling with its moral, racial, and spiritual identity. Yet I also write with a consciousness that readers may approach this work years from now, when today's crisis has become tomorrow's record.

This work has been for me, as a child of God but also as a preacher of the Good News of Jesus Christ — both a burden and a calling. It is not a historian's detached analysis, but a moral and theological reflection born out of prayer, conviction, and observation. While I do not claim to be a professional historian, I have given careful study to history, recognizing that nothing happens in a vacuum and that there is always cause and effect.

In my own journey, growing up in Durham, North Carolina, and educated in its public school system, I was not taught the fullness and the weightiness of America's history — which is also Black history. That story was minimized, sanitized, or left untold. Only later in life, around the age of thirty, did I come to understand that the civil rights struggles, the injustices, and the triumphs that shaped a generation were unfolding just years before and during my earliest years of life. That realization was not only academic; it was spiritual — a calling to trace the hand of God and the pattern of sin through the American experience.

This book, therefore, represents a continuum — the unbroken story of America's moral conflict, stretching from the "sacred sanction" of white supremacy to *The Rise of Trumpism* (2011-2025). It is written with the prayer that future generations — my children, my grandchildren, and all who come after — will understand how we arrived at this critical point in history and what God is saying to us through it.

I write not in condemnation but in compassion, that truth may bring reconciliation and healing. And it is my hope that this work will inspire readers, present and future alike, to act justly, love mercy, and walk humbly with God — even in a divided and uncertain world.

Preface

The Obama Effect, The Rise of Trumpism, and Christian Response was written out of both conviction and calling. This book was birthed from a desire to understand how a nation that once aspired toward moral clarity and democratic integrity could drift into such division, moral confusion, and political idolatry. I write not merely to document what has happened, but to bear witness to why it has happened — and to remind readers that God still speaks through the rise and fall of nations.

The contemporary events described herein are written as they unfold before my eyes. Yet I am acutely aware that those who read this work in the years to come will look back upon these same events as history. For this reason, this book occupies a sacred tension between the immediacy of the present and the long continuum of American history. What is present-day to me will one day be historical to you. But the moral truths that run through both moments remain unchanged: *"Righteousness exalts a nation, and sin is still a reproach to any people."*

This book builds upon the foundation of my earlier work — **Christianity, The White Man's Religion?** *The Great Lie, Reclaiming Biblical Truth* and **The Cause of Empire**: *Colonization, Civilization, Extermination, The Echoes That Built Our World.* In those writings, I sought to expose the roots of empire and the misuse of theology in the justification of oppression. In this present volume, I continue that pursuit by tracing how America's unhealed past converged with the present political moment — and how, beneath it all, lies a spiritual crisis that cannot be solved by politics alone.

My hope is that these reflections will serve as both a mirror and a lamp — revealing where we have been and illuminating where we must go. This book is not simply an analysis of history, but a moral appeal for repentance, reconciliation, and renewal under the authority of God's Word.

In short, by connecting the historical, political, and moral dimensions of America's story, this book seeks to provide both clarity and divine guidance — calling the church, the nation, and every reader to remember that no kingdom built on pride and oppression can stand forever, but the Kingdom of God endures — a world without end.

Introduction

America has always been a nation of promising contradictions. From her founding documents that proclaimed liberty while protecting slavery, to her self-image as a beacon of democracy even while practicing segregation, America's moral identity has been both luminous and shadowed. Each generation has wrestled with these contradictions — sometimes seeking to reconcile them, and other times reinforcing them through power, policy, and privilege.

The pressing question is not merely how did we arrive here, but how will we respond to the moral and political challenges before us. The nation stands at a spiritual and moral crossroads, testing whether the ideals once declared "self-evident" can survive the weight of hypocrisy, division, and deceit. The crisis before us is not only political; it is profoundly moral — a reflection of a nation's soul under judgment.

And yet this book is written within that living moment — the turning of the times. The words that follow are not composed from the quiet distance of hindsight but from within the noise, confusion, and moral testing of the present hour. While these events are unfolding before my eyes, I write with the awareness that others will read these same lines years, perhaps decades later, when the present has become history. In that sense, this work stands as both testimony and record — a reflection of now that speaks into what will be. For history is never dead; it moves through every generation, and each generation must answer anew what righteousness and truth require.

The Obama Effect, The Rise of Trumpism, and Christian Response explores the threads of history that connect past and present. It examines:

- The "sacred sanction" of white supremacy granted by European powers, and how this became the moral justification for conquest and colonization.

- The rise of pseudoscientific racial hierarchies in the 19th and 20th centuries, justifying slavery, segregation, and systemic exclusion.

- The enduring effects of systemic oppression and racial inequities on Black communities in America.

- The Obama effect, both as a symbol of progress and a catalyst for political backlash that shaped modern Trumpism.

- The rise of Trumpism as a political and cultural movement, with implications for governance, race relations, and the moral fabric of American democracy.

- The Christian response, grounded in biblical truth, prophetic witness, and the call to justice and reconciliation.

The book is structured to illuminate the historical, moral, and spiritual dimensions of America's racial and political struggle. It traces the evolution of ideas — from the theology of white supremacy to the political movements that have carried those ideas into the twenty-first century. It examines how empire-thinking has shaped American Christianity, and how faith communities can rediscover their prophetic voice in an age of confusion.

This is a work of reflection, revelation, and resolve. It is written with the conviction that truth must be spoken even when inconvenient, and that silence in the face of injustice is itself a moral failure. My prayer is that these pages will challenge, convict, and ultimately call the reader toward a deeper faith — one that sees through the illusions of power and rests in the eternal truth of God's kingdom.

CHAPTER 1

The Machine of Empire: An Engine Against African Americans and Indigenous Progress

To understand the forces that shaped the African American experience—and indeed, the world as it exists today—we must first turn our gaze backward, to the rise of European empires and colonization. The systems that worked against African American progress did not emerge in isolation; they were the calculated offspring of empire, conquest, and a worldview that exalted *whiteness* and power above righteousness.

Empire, in its most basic form, is the self-righteous extension of a nation's power through the domination of other lands and peoples. But in the European imagination of the fifteenth and sixteenth centuries, empire became more than political ambition—it was baptized in arrogance and justified by false theology — hence, moral duty. The "Age of Discovery" was not merely a quest for new trade routes or resources; it was a deliberate reshaping of the world according to the image and interests of Europe—whites.

Armed with superior weaponry, advanced naval technology, and disciplined military formations, European nations—Spain, England, France, the Netherlands and others—embarked upon global campaigns of conquest. Their cannons thundered against wooden defenses. Their muskets outranged spears and arrows. And their warships, propelled by sails and strategy, became floating empires, carrying the banner of conquest across the Atlantic and beyond. Indigenous nations, tribes, and kingdoms—many advanced in their own right—could not withstand the iron and gunpowder of Europe's armies.

This imbalance of military power was not accidental; it was the product of centuries of warfare within Europe itself. *Having honed their craft of destruction against one another, Europeans turned outward, convinced that their victories signified divine favor.* The false notion of European superiority took root and blossomed into a doctrine of global domination under the banner of so-called Christianity and Christ's cross. It wrongly and hypocritically declared through Scripture's perversion that those who wielded power must surely be chosen by God, and those who were conquered must somehow be inferior, destined for servitude or extinction.

Out of this toxic soil grew the ideology of social Darwinism—the belief that might makes right, that only the fittest deserve to survive, and that conquest is the natural order of humanity. Long before Darwin ever penned The Origin of Species, this worldview was already embedded in the European psyche. His later theories merely provided "scientific" justification for what empire had long practiced: the subjugation of the so-called weak by the strong, those wielding military might.

Colonization became the machinery through which empire maintained its grip. Lands were seized, resources extracted, and native populations displaced or destroyed. The cross and the sword marched side by side—missionaries often following soldiers, preaching salvation to those whose worlds had just been shattered. Kingdoms were dismantled, cultures erased, and people enslaved—all under the guise of civilization and Christian duty.

This was not the work of isolated men but of an organized system—a system that measured human worth by utility and skin color. The colonizers saw themselves not merely as conquerors but as so-called "civilizers." They justified their brutality with the language of progress, claiming to bring light to dark lands, even as they extinguished the lives of millions.

In this violent reshaping of the world, Africa became both a target and a tool. Its people were seen not merely as partners in trade, but as commodities in an emerging global market. The weapons that had subdued nations now enforced human bondage. This was the birth of chattel slavery—the economic and moral corruption that would define the Atlantic world for centuries to come.

The ideology of empire—rooted in pride, powered by violence, and sanctified by deception—laid the groundwork for every oppressive system that would later arise in America. The same spirit that justified colonization justified slavery. The same arrogance that crushed indigenous civilizations rationalized racial hierarchies. And the same blindness that mistook power for providence continues to shape the systems that work against African American progress today.

The Cost of Empire: Native Lands and Mexican Loss

The reach of empire did not end upon the shores of Africa. The same systems that trafficked in African bodies also trafficked in stolen land. Empire and colonization were not merely about wealth and resources—they were about possession. Possession of soil, possession of souls, possession of destiny itself. Nowhere was this more tragically revealed than in the lives of the Native peoples of the Americas and in the territorial dismemberment of Mexico.

When European settlers arrived upon the soil of the so-called "New World," they encountered nations already ancient, ordered, and wise in the stewardship of the earth. From the Iroquois Confederacy of the Northeast to the Cherokee and Creek in the South, from the Navajo and Apache of the deserts to the Sioux and Cheyenne of the Great Plains, the land pulsed with cultures rich in spiritual depth and ecological understanding. But the European eyes did not see nations—it saw opportunity. The colonizer's gaze was trained to see resources, not relationships; acres, not ancestors; conquest, not coexistence.

The English model of settler colonization differed from the Spanish and Portuguese empires before it. Whereas the Iberian powers often ruled through viceroys and extracted labor from Indigenous populations, English settlers came to replace the populations they found. They did not come merely to trade or govern—they came to inhabit; it was a hostile takeover. They brought families, farms, fences, and firearms. They arrogantly claimed frontier was their inheritance, and the people—"uncivilized people" who dwelled upon it were treated as obstacles to be removed.

The Theology of Empire

This ideology—*the theology of empire*, in the various forms or expressions it took, depending upon the empire or colonial nation, found spiritual justification in such ideology as the *Doctrine of Discovery*—a series of papal decrees and legal interpretations granting Christian explorers the "right" to claim lands not ruled by Christian princes. Under this twisted doctrine, the earth belonged to those powerful enough to seize it, provided they bore the name of Christ. It was theology weaponized; a gospel of greed dressed in sacred robes. The same cross that should have signified redemption became, for many Indigenous peoples, a marker of conquest.

What followed was a pattern of betrayal, forced displacement, and extermination. Entire tribes were wiped out by war, disease, and deceit. Treaties—hundreds of them—were made and broken as soon as they ceased to benefit the settler. The land hunger of empire was insatiable. From the Trail of Tears that drove the Cherokee from their ancestral lands to the decimation of the Plains nations under the U.S. Cavalry, the systems of colonization turned human lives into obstacles to progress. In the name of civilization, entire civilizations were destroyed!

The story extended beyond the Native nations to the lands of Mexico, which became another casualty of settler or empire's expansion. Following its independence from Spain in 1821, Mexico inherited vast territories stretching north into what would become California, Texas, Arizona, New Mexico, and beyond. But the young republic stood in the path of American settler ambition—a nation intoxicated with the notion of *Manifest Destiny*, the belief that it was divinely ordained to spread from the Atlantic to the Pacific.

This belief—half political theory, half religious conviction—gave delusional spiritual cover to imperial expansion. In 1846, under President James K. Polk, the United States provoked a war with Mexico, invading its territory and capturing its capital within two years. The Treaty of Guadalupe Hidalgo (1848) forced Mexico to surrender nearly half its land—more than 500,000 square miles—territory that would become some of the most valuable land in North America. Once again, the systems of conquest triumphed through deceit, power, and the myth of divine right.

For Native peoples and Mexicans alike, colonization was not a singular event—it was a continuing condition. Their histories were rewritten, their names erased, their faiths demonized, and their homelands parceled into property deeds. *Settler colonization worked not only through warfare but through law, policy, and religion.* It reshaped geography and memory alike, ensuring that those who once owned the land would soon labor upon it as strangers.

Empire thus laid a double foundation of injustice—land theft and human bondage. The colonization of Indigenous and Mexican lands and the enslavement of African bodies were not separate stories but chapters in the same book of human greed. One supplied the soil; the other supplied the labor. Together they formed the twin pillars upon which America would build its wealth—*and against which African Americans would struggle for centuries to come.*

The Early Bonds of the Oppressed

Before chattel slavery hardened into the brutal and racialized machine that would define the centuries to come, there existed a period in early colonial America when the boundaries between enslavement and servitude were still fluid. Africans, Native peoples, and impoverished Europeans found themselves bound together—not by shared privilege, but by shared suffering. The early seventeenth century was a time when survival blurred distinctions, and oppression was a common language spoken across color lines.

The earliest Africans brought to the English colonies, beginning in 1619, did not immediately enter a system of lifelong, hereditary slavery. Many were treated as indentured servants, bound for a term of years, much like their poor European counterparts. Some earned freedom after fulfilling their contracts; a few even acquired land or became craftsmen. But the shadow of something darker loomed just beyond the horizon.

Life in the colonies was harsh and uncertain. Disease, famine, and endless labor wore down all who toiled. On the plantations and in the fields, Native people, indentured Europeans, and Africans often worked side by side, united by necessity rather than status. Their shared misery bred an understanding—a fragile but real sense of common humanity. In that crucible of labor, bonds were formed that defied the rigid hierarchies later imposed by laws established by the white elite. They ate from the same meager rations, suffered under the same overseers, and often fled together into the wilderness, seeking freedom among Native nations who offered refuge from colonial tyranny.

The Native tribes, though themselves victims of conquest, sometimes extended a hand of compassion to escaped servants and Africans. They recognized in these strangers a familiar story: people torn from their homelands, stripped of dignity, and hunted by empire. Mutual need created moments of solidarity. In those early encounters, one can glimpse the possibility of a different America—an America where the oppressed might have stood together against the systems that dehumanized them all.

Among the poor white indentured servants, too, there was a growing awareness that their suffering mirrored that of the African laborers beside them. Though divided by origin and language, they shared the heavy yoke of exploitation. For many, bondage was a temporary condition, but the brutality of the experience carved deep resentment against the ruling planter class. The colonies were not a land of freedom for the poor; they were a land of hierarchy, where a few amassed wealth through the sweat and blood of the many.

At this early stage, race had not yet hardened into law. Social divisions were based more on class and circumstance than color. An African laborer and an English peasant could find common cause in their oppression. But as the economic systems of the colonies matured—particularly in tobacco-rich Virginia and Maryland—the ruling elite recognized the danger of such unity. A population bound together by shared suffering could also rise together in *shared rebellion*.

Thus, before the iron chains of racial slavery were forged, the colonies witnessed a fragile moment of human connection—poor whites, Africans, and Natives alike confronting a common oppressor. But the dream of solidarity among the downtrodden would soon be shattered. Fearful of the strength found in unity, the powerful began crafting laws and ideologies to divide. *They would redefine bondage not as a matter of class but as a matter of color.* Out of this deliberate division would emerge one of the most devastating inventions in human history: the engine of chattel slavery—the permanent enslavement of Africans and their descendants, justified by race and sanctioned by law.

The systems of empire, having already conquered lands, now turned to conquering bodies and souls. The transformation from indentured servitude to racial slavery marked the birth of a new order—an order that would shape the moral and material landscape of America for generations to come.

Bacon's Rebellion and the Birth of Whiteness

The fragile bonds that once united poor whites, Africans, and Native peoples in shared oppression shattered with a single event—Bacon's Rebellion of 1676. It was the moment the colonial project itself came under attack, not from foreign armies but from within. The uprising revealed the deep fractures of a society built upon exploitation, and in the aftermath, the ruling class—white elites, moved swiftly to ensure that such unity among the oppressed would never threaten their power again.

The rebellion began in Virginia under the leadership of Nathaniel Bacon, a wealthy but discontented planter. At first glance, the conflict appeared to be a quarrel among elites, a dispute between Bacon and Governor William Berkeley over how to handle conflicts with Native tribes. But beneath the surface ran a deeper current of unrest. Poor white farmers, landless laborers, and indentured servants—both African and European—joined forces under Bacon's banner, united in their anger toward the colonial elite. They burned Jamestown to the ground, turning their rage against the wealthy plantation owners who had hoarded land, monopolized trade, and treated them as disposable labor.

For the first time, the ruling class glimpsed the terrifying possibility of solidarity among the lower classes—a unity that transcended "race." The rebellion was crushed, but its message was unmistakable: *when the oppressed stand together, they threaten the entire structure of power.*

In the rebellion's aftermath, the colonial elite devised a plan not simply to suppress rebellion but to prevent unity from ever arising again. The solution was diabolical in its brilliance: *divide the oppressed along the line of color.* Thus began the deliberate construction of the racial hierarchy—a system designed not only to subjugate Africans but to elevate poor whites just enough to make them defenders, rather than challengers, of the existing order.

In the decades that followed, particularly in the early 1700s, Virginia and other colonies codified a series of laws that transformed servitude into chattel slavery—a permanent, hereditary condition reserved exclusively for Africans and their descendants. These laws stripped Black people of every legal right, denied them humanity, and bound their children and their children's children to perpetual servitude. At the same time, the same lawmakers extended privileges to poor whites, privileges not of wealth but of status.

White indentured servants, once treated no better than African laborers, were now promised access to land after their terms expired. They were given the right to bear arms, to testify in court, and to avoid corporal punishment for minor offenses. They could vote, serve in militias, and most importantly, they were told they were not Black. Even those who were not originally considered Anglo-Saxon—Irish, Scots, and other Europeans, as well, over the course of time, fair-skinned ethnic groups of other immigrants previously marginalized by colonial society—could embrace or claim whiteness and thereby gain access to these newly codified privileges. These benefits cost the elite nothing in material terms, but bought their allegiance with the cheapest of currencies—*the illusion and lie of superiority.*

This calculated manipulation is what later thinkers would call the *psychological wages of whiteness*; today it's viewed as *white privilege*. Though poor whites continued to struggle in poverty, they were given a new identity—one rooted not in their class but in their color. Their whiteness became their wage, a social currency that set them above even the most skilled and industrious Black laborer. This false sense of privilege created a hierarchy of belonging: even the poorest white man could now look upon himself as superior to every Black person, enslaved or free. The racial order thus replaced the class order, ensuring that the masses who once shared the same fields of labor would never again share the same cause.

These racial codes—passed and reinforced through the 1700s—became the foundation of *American racial ideology. They turned prejudice into policy and skin color into law.* Through these measures, the ruling class stabilized its power. They constructed a society in which the economic exploitation of African labor could continue unchecked because poor whites had been psychologically conscripted into the service of white supremacy. They had become both victims and enforcers of a system that benefitted only the few at the top.

The colonial elite had found the perfect formula: divide the laboring classes by race, elevate one group with status but not substance, and bind another with chains of law and ideology. The plantation system and the empire alike were secured not just by muskets and chains but by minds conditioned to see one's neighbor not as a brother in suffering but as a *racial other*. This mind manipulation and perversion of white souls continue to be hardwired into the hearts or DNA of many whites in America and beyond her borders.

The social construction of whiteness in the colonies would later be codified in federal law. The Naturalization Act of 1790 legally restricted U.S. citizenship to "free white persons," formalizing what had long existed as social privilege. While poor and marginalized Europeans had been able to claim whiteness socially in the colonial period, this law entrenched it legally, granting recognition, protection, and opportunity to those deemed white under the new federal system. In doing so, it reinforced a national hierarchy in which racial identity, not class or merit, determined access to citizenship, rights, and security. The act did not create whiteness—it merely cemented its authority in law, extending the privileges already enjoyed informally by poor whites while permanently excluding Africans and their descendants from equality.

Thus, out of rebellion arose a new order. The colonies would henceforth be defined by race rather than by class. The system that began as a means of labor control evolved into a total social structure—a racialized hierarchy sanctified by law, tradition, and even religion. From this structure emerged the full horror of chattel slavery, a system that would not only shape the American economy but deform its moral soul for generations to come. Currently, under Donald Trump's second term in office, we are seeing a subtle, but sure return to this engine of suppression and oppression, even so, the overt rise of "white supremacy and "white Christian Nationalism."

The Birth of Race Through Empire and Colonization

The invention of race did not emerge from biology or divine order but from the machinery of empire. European colonization, fueled by conquest and the pursuit of wealth, required both moral justification and social hierarchy to sustain itself. Thus, the myth of racial difference was born—not from truth, but from utility. It provided empire with a logic that allowed one people to dominate, enslave, and dispossess another while still calling itself "civilized."

From the earliest voyages of conquest, European powers—Spain, Portugal, England, and others—carried with them an ideology that fused Christianity with colonial ambition. They declared foreign lands "discovered," as if the people already living there did not exist, and justified domination under the banner of *divine sanction*. What began as imperial greed cloaked in religious language evolved into a full system of racial hierarchy. This ideology declared whiteness as the emblem of superiority and humanity, while Blackness and Indigeneity were marked as subhuman, fit for servitude or extermination.

In the American colonies, this racial logic took institutional form. Laws were written that divided those who labored together—poor Europeans, Native peoples, and Africans—and made the color of one's skin a measure of privilege or punishment. What had begun as a class-based colonial order hardened into a race-based one. Whiteness became currency; Blackness became crime. Through such laws, colonization birthed a new social reality in which power and identity were determined not by moral character, faith, or contribution, but by pigment and proximity to European likeness or skin color.

This racial construct, conceived in the heart of empire, became the scaffolding upon which chattel slavery, segregation, and white supremacy were later built. It was, and remains, the spiritual corruption of empire— a lie baptized in law and enforced by systems designed to preserve dominance.

The birth of race through empire and colonization did not remain an abstract theory or social distinction — it became the engine of enslavement itself. Once human worth was measured by color and codified in law, every brutality that followed could be justified as "natural order." The colonial mind, already conditioned by conquest and empire, now saw in the African body not a soul to be honored but a resource to be exploited. Thus, the ideology of racial hierarchy matured into a system of chattel slavery — one that demanded not merely submission, but the total dehumanization of an entire people. What began as the false science of difference became the theology of domination. It is to that dark and violent expression of racial ideology — the brutality and dehumanization tactics of enslavers — that we now turn.

Brutality and Dehumanization Tactics of Enslavers

As the colonial elite solidified the system of chattel slavery, the treatment of African people became not only economically exploitative but also ruthlessly violent. The plantation system was designed to extract labor, wealth, and obedience through terror and cruelty. The brutality was systematic, intended to break both body and spirit, leaving enslaved Africans with little chance to preserve their humanity within the confines of bondage.

The methods were relentless. Whippings, beatings, and mutilations were common punishments for the smallest infractions, and these acts were not random—they were calculated to instill fear or terror and ensure compliance. Enslaved people were denied any legal protection against such abuse, leaving overseers free to wield abusive power with absolute impunity. Families were torn apart as enslaved men, women, and children were sold at auction, often deliberately separated to undermine kinship and community bonds. This dislocation was a primary tool of psychological control, ensuring that even *natural affection became a site of vulnerability rather than resistance.*

The enslavement system also relied on dehumanizing rituals and restrictions. Enslaved Africans were prohibited from learning to read or write, cutting them off from knowledge, literacy, and empowerment. Religious instruction, when allowed, was often manipulated to justify submission rather than inspire liberation. Work hours were brutal, extending from sunup to sundown, often in hazardous conditions that caused injury or death. Clothing, food, and shelter were inadequate, leaving enslaved bodies exposed to disease, malnutrition, and extreme weather.

Even more insidious were the ways in which enslavers sought to control the mind and identity of the enslaved. Africans were stripped of their original names, languages, and cultural practices. African spiritual systems were suppressed, and European religious frameworks were imposed selectively, teaching obedience and discouraging resistance. By denying cultural memory and communal cohesion, enslavers aimed to sever the enslaved from any sense of dignity, history, or moral selfhood beyond the plantation.

Sexual Violence and Exploitation

The sexual violence and exploitation of enslaved women extended far beyond individual acts of sexual abuse by their slave owners. Entire plantations operated as "breeding farms," where enslaved women were forced to bear children to increase the labor force, ensuring the perpetuation of slavery across generations. These "breeding programs" treated human reproduction as property, reducing women and children to instruments of economic gain. Enslaved mothers often had no control over their pregnancies or family life, and infants were removed from their care to be sold or assigned to other laborers, deepening the trauma.

The forced inbreeding that sometimes resulted from these breeding farms produced long-term health disparities. Repeated intermarriage or sexual pairing among closely related enslaved individuals—whether enforced overtly or emerging from ignorance and limited social pools—led to an increase in both genetic disorders and developmental abnormalities, hence cognitive disorders.

Medical research supports that *consanguinity* can increase the likelihood of congenital conditions, physical deformities, and vulnerabilities to disease. In addition, the mental health consequences of such systemic violation—chronic stress, trauma, and learned helplessness—contributed to elevated rates of psychological disorders, depression, anxiety, and post-traumatic stress among enslaved populations. The combination of physical, cognitive, and mental health burdens underscores the multi-generational costs of the plantation system, with echoes still evident in descendants of enslaved people today.

Sexual violence and exploitation also targeted enslaved men in ways intended to humiliate, dominate, and break the human spirit. The practice known as "buck breaking" involved white men forcing themselves sexually upon enslaved Black men to establish control, humiliate them publicly, and dehumanize them before other enslaved individuals. This horrific tactic served both as a warning and a psychological weapon to prevent rebellion and resistance. White female slave owners, too, exercised sexual control over enslaved Black men, leveraging power and dominance for coercion or pleasure. These acts of sexual violence, whether by men or women, further stripped enslaved individuals of autonomy, dignity, and personhood.

Slave patrols and overseers enforced the system with terror. Patrolling bodies of the enslaved for escape, rebellion, or insubordination became institutionalized. Runaways were hunted, publicly whipped, branded, or executed as warnings. Resistance, when it occurred, was met with disproportionate violence to ensure that the wider enslaved population witnessed the consequences.

Through these measures, enslavers accomplished something far beyond economic exploitation—they created a system of *psychological domination*. Africans were not merely laborers; they were property, commoditized, and stripped of moral and social agency. This systematic brutality left *enduring scars* on the enslaved and their descendants, shaping not only the physical, cognitive, and emotional realities of those under bondage but also the moral fabric of the society that permitted such dehumanization.

The cruelty of chattel slavery was both material and spiritual, a dual assault on body and soul. By treating human beings as objects and animals, enslavers attempted to redefine what it meant to be human, imposing a worldview in which Black life was expendable, inferior, and entirely subject to white authority. This was not incidental or anomalous—it was central to the functioning of the plantation system and, by extension, the colonial economy itself.

Systems and Systemic Machinery That Oppress Blacks

The brutality and dehumanization of enslaved Africans were not isolated acts of cruelty—they were the product of a vast, interconnected system of oppression. Plantation hierarchies, colonial laws, slave patrols, and legal codifications worked in concert to maintain control over African bodies, minds, and spirits. These systems or machinery were designed not simply for short-term labor extraction but to entrench racial hierarchy, privilege whiteness, and normalize systemic domination.

This engine became self-perpetuating. Laws codified inequality; economic systems depended on racialized labor; social norms elevated white identity while denigrating African humanity. Even the terror of the overseer, the cruel spectacle of brutal punishment, and the dehumanizing rituals of "breeding" and sexual violence were not anomalies—they were essential components of a system engineered to maintain control and instill terror.

These systems were not merely historical—they are woven into the DNA of America. The horrors of chattel slavery, the deliberate destruction of families, bodies, and cultures, represent a form of ethno-genocide, or ethnocide, in which a people were systematically dehumanized, culturally erased, and exploited for economic and social gain. Even as centuries have passed, the residual effects of these systems remain embedded in institutions, policies, and social norms that continue to impact African Americans today.

Understanding these systems or systemic racism is critical. They provide the foundation for the persistent structural barriers and racialized ideologies that shape modern society. The oppression experienced during slavery was neither incidental nor temporary; it was a purposeful, enduring machinery designed to sustain inequality, and its influence echoes across generations.

Christian Response

As we reflect upon this chapter, we must confront a sobering truth: the sins of the past were not merely human failings—they were affronts to God's order and design for justice, mercy, and love. Scripture reminds us in Micah 6:8:

"He has shown you, O man, what is good; and what does the Lord require of you but to do justly, to love mercy, and to walk humbly with your God?"

The systems of oppression we have examined are antithetical to God's command. They sought to distort human dignity, fracture families, and deny the image of God inherent in every man, woman, and child. Yet Scripture calls the Church to witness, to speak truth, and to act in righteousness.

The work of justice is not merely political or social—it is spiritual. Acknowledgment of sin, repentance, and a commitment to restore what has been corrupted are the starting points for dismantling entrenched systems of oppression. Just as the Lord delivered His people from bondage in the days of old, so too must His people today stand against systemic injustice, advocate for the marginalized, and labor toward a society reflective of His holiness.

The history examined in this chapter should move us not to despair but to vigilance, courage, and faith-informed action. The legacy of slavery and the machinery of oppression call for the Church to be a light in the darkness—proclaiming truth, embodying mercy, and living as witnesses to the justice of God in a world still marred by human sin.

Let us approach this history with sorrow for the past, understanding for the present, and a steadfast commitment to God's righteousness for the future. The systems may be entrenched, but the Spirit of God calls us to dismantle injustice wherever it persists and to champion the dignity and life of every human soul.

CHAPTER 2

The Journey to Civil Rights, Yet the Struggle Continues

The Cornerstone Speech and Confederate Ideologies

In the shadow of the secession of Southern states from the Union, Alexander H. Stephens, vice president of the Confederate States of America, delivered what would become known as the Cornerstone Speech on March 21, 1861. In this address, Stephens laid bare the ideological foundations upon which the Confederacy was built—*a foundation deliberately rooted in white supremacy, the preservation of slavery, and the denial of African Americans' humanity and equality.*

Stephens declared that the Confederacy was founded upon "the great truth that the negro is not equal to the white man; that slavery—subordination to the superior race—is his natural and normal condition." In his perverted worldview, this racial hierarchy was not only natural but divinely sanctioned, an assertion designed to rationalize and legitimize the enslavement of millions. The speech crystallized a broader mindset among Southern leaders: that the political, economic, and social order must prioritize the power of whites and systematically oppress Blacks.

It is crucial to understand that Stephens' ideology did not emerge in a vacuum. Across the South, white politicians, planters, and intellectuals shared this belief in racial hierarchy and the so-called divine right of white elites to rule. Slavery was defended not only as an economic necessity but as a moral good, a civilizing mission, and, in the twisted logic of the day, a divinely ordained social order. This worldview gave rise to laws and customs designed to codify racial inequality, extending far beyond the formal institution of slavery itself.

Stephens' speech also reveals the psychological and cultural mechanisms used to sustain white dominance. By portraying African Americans as inherently inferior and incapable of self-determination, Southern leaders could justify extreme measures: forced labor, brutal physical punishment, and the denial of education, property rights, and political participation. These ideas were reinforced through sermons, educational systems, newspapers, and popular culture, creating a societal consensus that the natural order placed whites above Blacks.

Importantly, the Cornerstone Speech reflects the ideological engine that would resist African American advancement for generations. Even as the Civil War concluded and the Union sought to reconstruct a nation on the principles of liberty and equality, the ideas Stephens articulated persisted, morphing into subtler forms of structural and cultural resistance. *Segregation, the Lost Cause mythology, and the rise of organizations such as the United Daughters of the Confederacy* were all, in part, efforts to maintain the hierarchy Stephens championed.

In essence, Stephens' words and the broader Confederate ideology laid the intellectual and cultural groundwork for the systemic opposition to Black freedom and equality. They provided the philosophical justification for laws, social customs, and economic arrangements designed to deny African Americans the full fruits of their emancipation. The Cornerstone Speech serves as a stark reminder: the struggle for civil rights did not begin with Reconstruction nor end with legal amendments; it was, and continues to be, a battle against deeply embedded ideas and attitudes that have persisted across centuries.

The 13th, 14th, 15th Reconstruction Amendments as Legal Countermeasures

The close of the Civil War in 1865 did not end the battle over the soul of America—it merely shifted its battleground. The cannons fell silent, but the ideology Alexander H. Stephens so confidently proclaimed in his Cornerstone Speech continued to reverberate through the heart of the nation. The question before America was no longer whether slavery should exist, but whether the newly freed could ever truly be equal citizens in a nation built on their bondage.

In the aftermath of emancipation, Congress took up the monumental task of reconstructing a shattered Union and redefining freedom itself. The Reconstruction Amendments—the Thirteenth, Fourteenth, and Fifteenth— were not simply legal adjustments; they were moral declarations and constitutional countermeasures aimed at dismantling the ideological and institutional pillars of white supremacy.

The Thirteenth Amendment: Freedom Redefined (1865)

"Neither slavery nor involuntary servitude, except as a punishment for crime whereof the party shall have been duly convicted, shall exist within the United States…"

The Thirteenth Amendment, ratified in December 1865, legally abolished slavery. It was America's first great attempt to uproot the "cornerstone" of Stephens' Confederate ideology. But freedom was not merely the cessation of chains; it required the creation of systems that would ensure liberty's survival. The Amendment declared the end of slavery, but it left open the question of what would replace it—a question the South soon answered with *Black Codes, convict leasing, and sharecropping,* which reconstituted slavery's economic and social structure under new names.

Even so, the Thirteenth Amendment marked the first legal blow against the Confederate vision of racial hierarchy. It was the first brick removed from the edifice of white supremacy, signaling a national, but fragile, commitment to a new moral order.

The Fourteenth Amendment: Citizenship and Equal Protection (1868)

"All persons born or naturalized in the United States… are citizens of the United States and of the State wherein they reside."

The Fourteenth Amendment, ratified in 1868, confronted a deeper evil—the refusal to recognize Black humanity and citizenship. It granted birthright citizenship and promised equal protection under the law and due process to all persons, directly countering the Dred Scott decision of 1857, which had declared that no Black man had rights which a white man was bound to respect.

This Amendment sought to establish a constitutional floor beneath the feet of every American, ensuring that equality was not conditional upon race, region, or class. But its promise would be tested almost immediately. States found new methods of resistance—*Jim Crow laws, discriminatory policing, and voter suppression*—to deny African Americans the very rights the Fourteenth Amendment enshrined. Still, this Amendment became the cornerstone of modern civil rights jurisprudence, invoked in nearly every major legal battle for equality since its ratification.

The Fifteenth Amendment: The Struggle for the Ballot (1870)

"The right of citizens of the United States to vote shall not be denied or abridged… on account of race, color, or previous condition of servitude."

Ratified in 1870, the Fifteenth Amendment was designed to secure the most powerful instrument of freedom—the vote. For African Americans, the ballot represented both the symbol and substance of citizenship. It was the means by which the formerly enslaved could influence laws, challenge injustice, and protect their newly won rights.

Yet even before the ink dried, Southern legislatures devised schemes to undermine it: literacy tests, poll taxes, grandfather clauses, and outright terror through organizations like the Ku Klux Klan. What was written as a constitutional right became, in practice, a battleground soaked in intimidation and blood. The Fifteenth Amendment established the principle of voting equality; the struggle to make that principle real would continue well into the twentieth century—and beyond.

The 24th and 26th Amendments: Expanding the Promise of Democracy

The 24th Amendment (1964) abolished the poll tax in federal elections—a tool long used to suppress poor Black voters in the South. This Amendment emerged as part of the broader Civil Rights Movement, reflecting how deeply the nation had resisted the full realization of the Fifteenth Amendment's intent.

A decade later, the 26th Amendment (1971) lowered the voting age to 18, a recognition that those called to serve and die for their country in Vietnam deserved a voice in its democracy. While not exclusively a racial amendment, its passage continued the broader trajectory of expanding democratic inclusion—an ideal born from the same Reconstruction impulse that sought to bring African Americans fully into the civic body.

Together, these Amendments stand as America's moral rebuttal to the Cornerstone ideology. Where Stephens and his peers envisioned a republic built upon racial hierarchy, these constitutional measures sought to erect a new foundation—one grounded in liberty, equality, and justice. Yet, their very necessity revealed the depth of the disease they sought to cure. Each Amendment was both a declaration of victory and an acknowledgment of resistance, a legislative proclamation that freedom could not coexist with oppression.

Still, these Amendments alone could not erase the deeply embedded cultural and economic structures of racism. The ink on the parchment was barely dry before new systems arose to circumvent their intent. The next section will explore precisely that enduring opposition—the persistence of Confederate ideology in new forms of racial control and exclusion.

Timeline: The Journey of Struggle and Resistance

Codification and Evolution of Whiteness in America, 1600s – Early Colonial Period. Early colonies had a mix of European indentured servants and African people. Race-based distinctions were not initially fully rigid, but over time, laws began privileging Europeans over Africans and Indigenous peoples.

Key example: Virginia (1662) – Children inherited the status of the mother; enslaved status became permanent for African descendants, distinguishing them from poor white servants. 1670s–1700s – Legal Codification of Race, Virginia Slave Codes (1660s–1705): Restricted the rights of Black people, prohibited interracial marriage, and legally enforced slavery.

Maryland (1691): Black people could not own land or bear arms; free whites had privileges. *This period established whiteness as a legal and social category*, giving white colonists rights denied to Black and Indigenous people.

1700s–1800s – Citizenship and Privilege, Naturalization Act (1790): Limited U.S. citizenship to "free white persons," excluding Africans, Indigenous people, and non-European immigrants. Slavery expanded in the South; white elites codified racial hierarchies in law, politics, and society.

Post-Civil War (1865–1877), 13th Amendment (1865): Abolished slavery. 14th Amendment (1868): Defined citizenship and equal protection under law. 15th Amendment (1870): Gave Black men the right to vote. Despite these amendments, Southern states implemented Jim

Crow laws, literacy tests, poll taxes, and segregation, effectively maintaining white privilege and dominance.

Early 1900s – Immigration and Whiteness Immigration Acts (1920s): Favored Northern and Western European immigrants as "desirable whites," restricting Asians, Africans, and others. Whiteness became tied to nationality and culture, not just skin color.

Mid–Late 20th Century – Civil Rights Era Civil Rights Act (1964): Outlawed discrimination in public accommodations, employment, and education. Voting Rights Act (1965): Enforced the 15th Amendment; attempted to dismantle barriers to Black voting. Despite legal equality, systemic advantages for whites persisted, including housing segregation, education disparities, and economic opportunities.

Late 20th – Early 21st Century, Whiteness evolved from a legal category to a structural advantage (what we now call "white privilege"). Benefits include easier access to education, wealth accumulation, and political influence, often unseen or normalized in culture. Present day, structural inequalities continue, including disparities in wealth, criminal justice, health, and political power. Efforts like anti-racism education, equity policies, and reparative programs sought to address the long-lasting effects of codified whiteness. But now, the country under the *strongman tactics* of Donald Trump is being systematically dismantled—the Second Redemption Era or Neo-Reconstruction backlash has once again risen under Trumpism.

Initially, whiteness in America was legally codified to ensure privilege and maintain racial hierarchy. Over centuries, it evolved into a cultural and systemic advantage, which persists even when explicit laws enforcing racial inequality have been abolished.

So it was, codification happened, and the meaning of whiteness shifted from legal status to broader social, economic, and cultural power. Sadly, this ideology of white privilege remains intact in the hearts of more than a few whites who view themselves as Christian, a delusion far removed from the biblical message—*we are all one and equal under God who created mankind.*

Ongoing Resistance and White Backlash

The ink that freed the slave had hardly dried before the old order rose again in new garments. The fall of the Confederacy may have ended slavery as a legal institution, but it did not end the arrogant and spiritually corrupt mindset that gave birth to it. From the ashes of defeat, the ideology of white supremacy adapted, reshaped, and reasserted itself—first through terror, then through law, and eventually through culture and custom. The same defiant spirit that Alexander H. Stephens had immortalized in his Cornerstone Speech continues to haunt the nation's conscience.

The Reconstruction Era: 1865-1877

The Reconstruction Era emerged in the wake of the Civil War, a period in which the United States faced the immense task of rebuilding not only its infrastructure but also its social and political order. For African Americans, Reconstruction initially held the promise of freedom and the restoration of human dignity. As stated previously, the abolition of slavery through the 13th Amendment (1865) legally freed millions of formerly enslaved people, while the 14th Amendment (1868) granted citizenship and promised equal protection under the law. The 15th Amendment (1870) further sought to enfranchise Black men, giving them the constitutional right to vote.

Again, despite these monumental legal victories, the realities on the ground were far harsher. Freed people faced enormous challenges as white supremacist structures, deeply embedded in Southern society, sought to undermine the progress of Reconstruction. Systems such as sharecropping and tenant farming trapped many African Americans in cycles of economic dependence and exploitation, replacing physical bondage with financial and social servitude. This economic machinery, coupled with Black Codes and the rise of homegrown terrorists like the Ku Klux Klan, violently suppressed African Americans' newfound rights, often through intimidation and murder.

Politically, African Americans made significant gains during Reconstruction. They were elected to local, state, and even federal offices, creating a brief but profound window of Black political empowerment. However, these gains were fiercely contested by white supremacists who used violence, fraud, and systemic disenfranchisement to roll back progress. By the end of Reconstruction in 1877, the withdrawal of federal troops from the South effectively ended federal enforcement of Black civil rights, ushering in the Jim Crow era, this new hellish and oppressive period of legalized segregation and entrenched racial hierarchy that would persist for decades—hence the "Redemptive Era".

The promise to freed Blacks of 40 acres and a mule and 400,000 acres of land along the coast of South Carolina, Georgia and Florida was revoked; land that had been given to Blacks was taken back by whites, no thanks to President Andrew Jackson, after the assassination of President Lincoln.

Spiritually and socially, the African American community responded to these challenges with remarkable resilience. The church was the central institution of Black life, providing not only spiritual sustenance but also education, social organization, and leadership. Freed people built schools, churches, and civic organizations, sowing the seeds of a culture and community that would later sustain the civil rights movement. Yet the persistent threats of violence, economic oppression, and systemic exclusion reinforced the long road ahead, shaping the collective consciousness that would fuel later struggles for equality.

In short, the Reconstruction Era was both a time of hope and a great betrayal by the government. It demonstrated the possibility of racial justice while revealing the depth and persistence of systemic opposition to African American progress. The failures and lessons of Reconstruction would directly mobilize and inform the Great Migration and the Renaissance Period, both of which became critical stages in the fight for civil rights during the mid-20th century.

Reconstruction Undermined

During Reconstruction (1865–1877), federal efforts to rebuild the South and protect Black rights met immediate and violent resistance. Blacks established schools, churches, and civic organizations, and for a brief moment, democracy blossomed in Southern soil. Black men were elected to public office—over 2,000 African Americans held local, state, and federal positions, including Hiram Revels and Blanche K. Bruce in the U.S. Senate.

Yet white southerners saw these advancements as an existential threat. The Ku Klux Klan and other white terror organizations emerged as instruments of fear, using lynching, arson, and intimidation to reassert control. The Compromise of 1877, which ended federal Reconstruction, effectively abandoned Black citizens to the mercy of their former enslavers. Without the protection of federal troops, the South quickly moved to reverse the gains of freedom through their new systems of control, as noted—Black Codes, debt peonage, land theft and sharecropping— restoring the racial order in all but name.

Jim Crow and the Legalization of Segregation

The dawn of the Jim Crow era in the late 19th century marked the formalization of racial segregation. What had begun as local customs became codified law. In 1896, the Supreme Court's decision in Plessy v. Ferguson sanctioned the doctrine of *"separate but equal,"* providing constitutional cover for decades of systemic discrimination.

Under Jim Crow, African Americans were denied access to decent schools, fair wages, and political representation. Entire communities were relegated to the margins of American life— segregated "public" spaces, segregated cars, segregated schools, segregated neighborhoods, and segregated futures.

But even more sinister was the cultural propaganda that reinforced it. The myth of the "Lost Cause," propagated by groups such as the *United Daughters of the Confederacy*, romanticized the Old South as a noble civilization destroyed by Northern aggression. *They rewrote history books, erected Confederate statues, and celebrated national traitors as heroes.* This ideological campaign sought not only to vindicate the Confederacy but to legitimize white supremacy as Southern tradition.

Lynching and the Culture of Terror

White backlash was not confined to laws—it was also a reign of terror. Between 1882 and 1968, more than 4,700 documented lynchings took place in the United States, the majority targeting African Americans. These public spectacles of violence—often announced in newspapers and attended by crowds to include white families and their children—were designed to terrorize entire communities.

Activists like Ida B. Wells risked their lives to expose the barbarity of lynching, calling it what it truly was: racial control by terror. Wells' work laid the moral groundwork for later civil rights activism by linking America's racial violence to its hypocrisy before God and the world.

The lynching era revealed the depth of white fear: fear that the enslaved would become equal, that the laborer would rise to ownership, that the oppressed would learn to read and lead. It was not hatred alone that fueled white backlash—it was the terror of equality.

The Great Migration: 1916-1970

In the decades following Reconstruction and the institutionalization of Jim Crow, African Americans faced persistent economic, political, and social oppression in the South. The evil and oppressive systemic racial structures of sharecropping, tenant farming, violence, and disenfranchisement created a suffocating environment, leaving millions with limited avenues for advancement. In response, a monumental movement began — the mass exodus of African Americans from the rural South to the urban North, Midwest, and West, known as the Great Migration. Over six million African Americans would relocate during this period, seeking economic opportunity, political freedom, and personal safety.

The migration unfolded in two major waves. The first wave (1916–1940) was driven largely by labor shortages in Northern industries during World War I. Factories, railroads, and steel mills called for workers, and the promise of higher wages and safer conditions lured southern Black families to cities such as Chicago, Detroit, Cleveland, and New York. The second wave (1941–1970) corresponded with World War II and postwar industrial expansion, as African Americans continued to flee entrenched racial violence in the South and sought better social and economic prospects.

The Great Migration transformed the cultural, economic, and political landscape of the United States. Northern cities became hubs of African American life, fueling new urban communities, institutions, and networks that fostered resilience and creativity. African Americans excelled in politics, science, medicine, philosophy, and the arts, producing inventions and innovations that not only advanced the African American community but also contributed to the nation and reverberated across the globe. Notable achievements include:

1. Garrett Morgan – inventor of the three-position traffic light and the gas mask.

2. George Washington Carver – pioneer in agricultural science and crop rotation techniques, introducing hundreds of uses for peanuts, sweet potatoes, and other crops.

3. Madam C.J. Walker – entrepreneur and inventor of hair care products for Black women, creating the first American female self-made millionaire.

4. Granville T. Woods – "Black Edison," who patented devices for railways, including the multiplex telegraph and improvements to the telephone.

5. Lonnie Johnson – engineer and inventor of the Super Soaker water gun, contributing to both toy innovation and energy systems.

6. Otis Boykin – inventor of electrical resistors used in computers, radios, and pacemakers.

7. Marie Maynard Daly – first African American woman to earn a Ph.D. in chemistry in the U.S., contributing to cardiovascular research.

8. Percy Julian – chemist who synthesized important medicinal compounds, including synthetic cortisone and steroids.

9. Benjamin Banneker – mathematician and astronomer, known for designing the first clock made in America and for contributions to early surveying.

10. Elijah McCoy – inventor of lubrication systems for steam engines, giving rise to the phrase "the real McCoy" for quality inventions.

These accomplishments and many others illustrate that African Americans were not passive observers of history but active innovators and leaders whose contributions shaped modern life far beyond their communities, impacting the nation and the world.

Yet, migrants often encountered racial discrimination, segregated housing, and labor exploitation even in the North. This was when redlining, restrictive covenants, and overcrowded neighborhoods marked the new urban experience, while the promise of opportunity was tempered by systemic racial barriers. Still, African Americans persevered, building strong churches, schools, and civic institutions that became the backbone of urban communities.

Spiritually and socially, the migration reinforced community cohesion, cultural identity, and resilience. These cities incubated artistic and intellectual movements, most notably the Harlem Renaissance, which celebrated African American creativity and intellect while asserting racial dignity in the face of ongoing oppression.

The Great Migration was not merely a movement of bodies across geography; it was a migration of hope, resistance, and self-determination. It laid the foundation for the mid-20th-century civil rights movement, as a newly urbanized, politically conscious, and culturally empowered African American population began to demand justice, equality, and recognition on a national and international scale.

The Great Migration and New Forms of Resistance

And so it was that the early 20th century brought a new chapter in Black resistance. Millions of African Americans fled the rural and segregated South. They carried with them not only the memory of oppression but also the determination to build new lives beyond the reach of Jim Crow.

However, even in the North, racism followed. Housing covenants, redlining, employment discrimination, and racial violence—such as the Chicago Race Riot of 1919—proved that white backlash was not a regional sickness but a national one. Yet the migration also birthed powerful cultural movements: the Harlem Renaissance, the rise of Black newspapers, and new institutions of advocacy such as the NAACP (1909), the National Urban League (1910), and the Brotherhood of Sleeping Car Porters (1925), led by A. Philip Randolph.

Each of these institutions became spiritual and strategic training grounds for the modern Civil Rights Movement.

The Renaissance Period: Cultural and Intellectual Awakening

The influx of African Americans into Northern cities during the Great Migration not only reshaped the urban landscape but also ignited a cultural and intellectual revolution. Known most prominently as the Harlem Renaissance in the 1920s and 1930s, this period was marked by a profound assertion of African American identity, creativity, and dignity. Artists, writers, musicians, scholars, and thinkers began to reclaim their narrative, producing works that celebrated the richness of Black culture and challenged pervasive racial stereotypes.

Figures such as Langston Hughes, Zora Neale Hurston, Claude McKay, and Countee Cullen used literature and poetry to explore the African American experience, weaving together themes of resilience, struggle, and hope. In music, jazz and blues exploded onto the national stage, with icons like Duke Ellington, Louis Armstrong, and Bessie Smith transforming

American music and influencing culture worldwide. These artistic achievements were not mere entertainment; they were acts of spiritual and cultural defiance, asserting the humanity, intellect, and beauty of a people long demeaned by systemic oppression.

The Renaissance also fostered philosophical and intellectual leadership, as African American scholars and activists sought to analyze and confront the social and political realities of their time. Organizations such as the NAACP, along with thinkers like W.E.B. Du Bois, emphasized education, civil rights, and civic engagement, linking cultural production with political activism. The period nurtured a generation that believed in the power of art, thought, and knowledge as instruments of Black liberation and social transformation.

Crucially, the Renaissance revealed the interconnectedness of cultural and political progress. The pride, visibility, and intellectual vigor generated during this period laid the groundwork for the civil rights activism of the mid-20th century. African Americans, having established robust communities in Northern cities, leveraged these cultural and intellectual gains to demand legal rights, political participation, and social justice in a nation that had long denied them full citizenship.

Spiritually, the Renaissance was a reaffirmation of the divine creativity within the African American community. Churches, literary societies, and artistic circles became spaces where faith, intellect, and cultural expression intertwined, reinforcing the resilience, hope, and moral fortitude necessary to challenge entrenched injustice. The period demonstrated that freedom is not solely political but also cultural, spiritual, and intellectual, and that the fight for civil rights would require a holistic vision of liberation.

In sum, the Renaissance Period was both a celebration of African American achievement and a strategic preparation for the struggle ahead. It amplified the voices of a people long silenced, provided a foundation for social and political mobilization, and contributed indelibly to the moral and cultural fabric of the nation. It was this convergence of migration, cultural awakening, and intellectual assertion that paved the way for the monumental civil rights victories of 1955 through 1965.

White Backlash in the 20th Century

As African Americans gained ground—through war service, education, and civic engagement—white America's resistance evolved yet again. The mid-20th century saw massive resistance to desegregation following Brown v. Board of Education (1954). Southern politicians issued the Southern Manifesto, pledging to resist integration "by all lawful means." Governors like Orval Faubus in Arkansas and George Wallace in Alabama became symbols of defiance, standing in schoolhouse doors and shouting, "Segregation now, segregation tomorrow, segregation forever!"

The backlash was not confined to the South. In cities like Boston, Chicago, and Los Angeles, white mobs protested school integration and housing equality. This era revealed that racism was not just a Southern sin—it was an American structure, deeply woven into the nation's DNA, its political, economic, and psychological fabric.

Faith and the Counter-Narrative

Yet, amid the storm of backlash, the Black Church became the sanctuary of resilience. Ministers, lay leaders, and ordinary believers grounded their activism in faith. They preached a gospel of liberation rooted in Scripture —**"Let justice roll down like waters, and righteousness like a mighty stream"** (Amos 5:24).

This moral foundation would become the wellspring of the Civil Rights Movement. It gave theological legitimacy to the struggle for justice and framed equality not merely as a political demand but as a divine mandate.

The Struggle Before the March

By the time America reached the mid-20th century, the foundations for the Civil Rights Movement had already been laid in the blood and faith of generations. The Reconstruction Amendments had written equality into law, but white grievance and backlash had written inequality into practice. From the ashes of Reconstruction through the terror of Jim Crow, from the flight of the Great Migration to the awakening of the Black Church, every phase of the African American journey and struggle carried the echo of a single cry: *freedom must be more than words.*

The next section—"Link to the Road to Civil Rights"—will trace how these cumulative struggles converged into the moral revolution of the 1950s and 1960s, when faith and protest joined hands to confront America's unfinished work.

Link to the Road to Civil Rights

The mid-20th century did not create the struggle for civil rights—it revealed its culmination. Every march, every sit-in, and every sermon from the pulpit was the flowering of seeds planted generations before. From the smoldering remains of Reconstruction, through the terror of lynching and Jim Crow, the Black freedom struggle moved like a river, winding but unstoppable, carrying both the memory of pain and the hope of redemption.

The Long Continuum of Struggle

The Civil Rights Movement of 1955–1965 was not an isolated decade—it was the visible eruption of a centuries-long undercurrent of faith, resilience, and resistance. The abolitionist preachers (both Blacks and whites), the freedom fighters of Reconstruction, the sharecroppers who risked everything to vote, the mothers who walked to work rather than ride segregated buses—all formed the spiritual genealogy of that movement.

The Montgomery Bus Boycott (1955–1956), the Greensboro sit-ins (1960), the Freedom Rides (1961), the March on Washington (1963), and Selma's Bloody Sunday (1965) were not spontaneous events. They were the inevitable outcome of a people who refused to be oppressed any longer and die in silence.

When Rosa Parks sat, she was standing in a lineage that stretched from the plantations to the protest line. When Dr. King spoke of a dream, he was echoing the prophets before him and the enslaved who had prayed, "How long, O Lord?"

Faith as the Engine of Freedom

The Black Church became the moral compass and mobilizing center of the Civil Rights era. Churches served as meeting halls, printing presses, legal aid centers, and sanctuaries for courage. From pulpits rose a theology that declared God on the side of the oppressed, echoing the words of Exodus:

"I have surely seen the affliction of My people which are in Egypt, and have heard their cry by reason of their taskmasters; for I know their sorrows" (Exodus 3:7).

This conviction—that the struggle for justice was not merely constitutional but covenantal—gave the movement its spiritual power. The movement was, at its heart, a moral confrontation between the kingdom of God and the empire of man.

The Civil Rights Legacy and Its Continuing Assault: The Road Yet Unfinished

This hopeful era, the Civil Rights Acts of 1964 and the Voting Rights Act of 1965 represented monumental victories, but they did not complete the journey. They marked milestones along a continuing road—a road still lined with barriers and resistance.

Dr. King, before his death, warned that the movement had merely exposed the roots of the problem; the deeper work would be *to change the soul of America*. He said, "We must rapidly begin the shift from a 'thing-oriented' society to a 'person-oriented' society."

Today, the unfinished work remains. The same questions that haunted America in 1865, in 1965, still echo in 2025:

- Who belongs?
- Who counts?
- Who is free?
- Who is equal?

The road to civil rights was never a ten-year march—it is a moral pilgrimage that stretches across generations, from the plantation to the pulpit, from Selma to today's voting booths.

A Continuing Call to Conscience

The prophetic words of Scripture continue to ring true:

"Righteousness exalteth a nation: but sin is a reproach to any people" (Proverbs 14:34).

Until righteousness becomes the foundation of our national life, the reproach of racism, inequality, and hatred will remain. The Civil Rights Movement did not end with King's dream; it continues wherever the Church stands against injustice and wherever believers live out the gospel that declares *all are made in the image of God.*

The road to civil rights, then, is not merely historical—it is eternal. It is the journey of a people, and a nation, learning—often painfully—that true greatness is not found in power, but in justice.

Yet, as history bears witness, every step forward toward freedom in America has been met by a countermovement determined to pull the nation backward. The same supremacist and divisive spirit that once resisted Reconstruction now reemerges under new names, new slogans, and new laws—each designed to reassert control and maintain the racial hierarchy that the gospel of Christ condemns.

In recent years (mid-2000s and currently), we have seen a deliberate and highly organized effort to roll back the hard-won gains of the Civil Rights era—in voting rights, women's rights, educational opportunity, and social equality. Under the banner of "Make America Great Again," the MAGA movement—Trumpism has cloaked racial grievance and white patriarchal nostalgia in patriotic rhetoric, seeking to resurrect an older social order that privileges whiteness and male dominance.

Through voter suppression laws, gerrymandering, and judicial rollback, this modern movement mirrors the tactics of the post-Reconstruction South, when the legal system was manipulated to strip Black citizens of their newly acquired rights. Court decisions, most notably Shelby County v. Holder (2013), weakened the Voting Rights Act of 1965, allowing states once monitored for discrimination to reimpose restrictive voting laws that disproportionately impact African Americans.

A parallel assault has taken place in the realm of education and opportunity. The recent Supreme Court decision striking down Affirmative Action (2023) marks yet another reversal of the moral progress won through decades of struggle. Affirmative Action *was not a handout—it was a corrective, an acknowledgment that racial injustice had systematically denied African Americans access to higher education and employment.* Its abolition under the guise of "colorblind fairness" is a return to the deceptive logic of the Jim Crow era: that equality can exist without justice, and that history's wounds no longer matter.

This "colorblind" rhetoric has become a tool of modern racism—subtle, sanitized, and socially acceptable. It denies the enduring reality of systemic oppression while reinforcing the privileges that continue to advantage white Americans. It is the language of evasion, the pretense that racial inequity can be ignored because it is uncomfortable to confront.

Meanwhile, Black women, long the moral backbone of the freedom struggle, now face renewed assaults on both racial and gender fronts. The rollback of reproductive rights, the undermining of voting protections, and the silencing of women's voices in leadership all point toward a resurgent patriarchal order intent on reclaiming lost dominance.

Whereas I have chosen to make mention of the matter of reproductive rights, it does not mean I'm in support of blanket abortions. In the case of rape, or a mother's health or life being at risk, I allow exceptions. There may be other sensitive and extenuating circumstances that may also justify such an allowance.

Trumpism, as both a political and cultural force, channels the old Confederate spirit into the modern age—disguising hierarchy as nationalism, and prejudice as patriotism. Its goal, like that of the postbellum South, is not merely to influence elections but to reshape the national narrative, to recast equality as threat and justice as overreach.

The pattern is unmistakable: from the end of Reconstruction to the rise of Jim Crow, from the dismantling of Affirmative Action to the weakening of voting rights, each regression reflects a single truth—America's struggle with race is not confined to its past; it is woven into its present. The nation's laws may evolve, but the spiritual sickness of racial superiority remains deeply rooted in the American soul.

The struggle for equality in America has never existed in isolation; every advance toward justice has provoked a counter-movement determined to restore the old order. The same spirit that animated the defenders of slavery and segregation now resurfaces in new political garments, additionally cloaked in the rhetoric of "white evangelical Christian values," "tradition," "liberty," and "states' rights." Yet beneath these slogans lies the same enduring anxiety — the fear of a transformed social hierarchy where power is shared and justice is impartial.

As the gains of the Civil Rights Movement face erosion through legislation, judicial rulings, and cultural revisionism, the question for the present generation mirrors that of those who marched in Selma and Montgomery: Will America honor its promises, or will it retreat once more behind the color line? Currently (2025), the push is in the direction of a dangerous white supremacist redux or revival.

Christian Response

The righteous Christian faith has always stood at a crossroads with empire, oppression, and the pursuit of human dignity. In every generation, believers have faced the test of whether to conform to the moral blindness of the age or to bear witness to the liberating truth of the Gospel. The road to civil rights was not only a political movement — it was a spiritual reckoning. For the African American church, faith in Christ was both shield and sword: a shield against despair and a sword against injustice.

When earthly systems codified inequality, the Scriptures declared that **all humanity is made in the image of God** (Genesis 1:27). When courts and constitutions denied full citizenship, the cross proclaimed divine citizenship in a kingdom **"that shall not be moved"** (Hebrews 12:28). The faith of those who marched, prayed, and endured was rooted not in social theory but in sacred conviction — that *Christ's redemption was total, and therefore it must confront total oppression.*

The prophets of the Old Testament stood against kings and nations that oppressed the poor, silenced justice, and perverted righteousness. Likewise, the Church in America is called to expose the powers that still resist the freedom of God's image-bearers. The Apostle Paul reminds the Church that **"we wrestle not against flesh and blood, but against principalities and powers"** (Ephesians 6:12). These "powers" take form today in racialized systems, economic exploitation, and political idolatry that disguise themselves as patriotism or national revival.

The Christian or righteous children of God must see through these deceptions. For when any ideology exalts one race, class, or gender above another, it becomes anti-Christ in spirit, opposing the very reconciliation the Gospel proclaims. The message of Christ compels believers to dismantle false hierarchies and to rebuild communities upon justice, mercy, and truth. **"He hath shewed thee, O man, what is good; and what doth the Lord require of thee, but to do justly, and to love mercy, and to walk humbly with thy God?"** (Micah 6:8).

The modern Church must also repent where it has been silent. Too often, pulpits have blessed injustice with neutrality, calling it peace. But Christ did not die to make men comfortable; He died to make them new. Silence in the face of sin is complicity. The Gospel, when rightly preached, is revolutionary — it dethrones pride, confronts privilege, and levels humanity at the foot of the cross.

In this generation, as in the civil rights struggle, the Christian must again take the mantle of moral leadership. The Church cannot retreat behind denominational walls while democracy crumbles under the weight of greed, racism, and deceit. Faith must not be privatized; it must become incarnate — walking, speaking, and advocating for the least of these (Matthew 25:40).

The road to civil rights was paved not only with legislation but with prayer, perseverance, and prophetic faith. That same faith must now confront new forms of bondage — mass incarceration, economic inequality, the assault on voting rights, and the resurgence of white Christian nationalism masquerading as revival. Yet, even now, the Word of God endures: **"The light shineth in darkness; and the darkness comprehended it not"** (John 1:5).

To be Christian in this hour is to stand with Christ against every Pharaoh, every Herod, and every Caesar that demands allegiance to systems of oppression. It is to live out the commandment that love is stronger than hate, truth mightier than lies, and justice more enduring than empire. The church that forgets this ceases to be the church. The believer who lives this truth becomes part of the divine resistance that no earthly power can overthrow.

CHAPTER 3

Freedom Rising: Hope, Sacrifice, and The Blood of the Movement

As a young father in my late twenties, raising two young sons—Mario and Desmond—I began to experience the necessity to understand the story of my African ancestry and the true history of this nation called America. I needed to become more informed about "Black History," which is inseparable from America's History, for myself as well as for my sons.

Politically, I seem to recall that the climate was racially charged under the leadership of Republican President George H. W. Bush, but it was perhaps during the presidency of Ronald Reagan, also a Republican, that this desire to know more about African American history began to take root. I realized that what I had been taught in the public school system was woefully incomplete. The history of slavery, Reconstruction, and the Civil Rights Movement was either glossed over or told through such a sanitized lens that I retained little of it.

The first unfiltered lesson or history I received about my African ancestors came not from a classroom, but from a television screen. In 1977, I was twelve years old when I first saw the mini-series Roots. This story was based on the ancestors of Alex Haley. His book and the television saga tell the story of how his family was stolen from Africa and trafficked to America, and enslaved. Alex's family story was not unique to his ancestors; it was the story of every African forcefully brought to America, shackled in and under the horrible conditions found on slave ships bound to the Americas and Caribbean Islands and elsewhere.

Those scenes of men, women and children chained, whipped, sold, and stripped of their homeland and dignity left a lasting mark upon my heart and psyche. For the first time, I saw history as deeply personal. The lives portrayed on that screen represented my ancestors—their suffering, their pain, their endurance, their faith. That cinematic lesson became the origin and foundation of my later pursuit to uncover truth, to study the past, and to seek God's wisdom for how His people might move toward understanding such unprecedented evil, but also to pursue reconciliation.

It was in December of 1992, at the age of twenty-seven, that I was licensed to preach the Gospel of Jesus Christ—the good news that offers forgiveness, reconciliation, and healing to a broken and lost world. As I stood behind the pulpit, having begun the process of furthering my learning and understanding that I may be able to prophetically proclaim God's *Word* that I began to understand over time, how vital it was to confront the bigotry and racism that had long divided the people of God. The Gospel calls for unity, not separation; for compassion, not contempt. Only through an honest reckoning with America's past sins can the Church fully preach Christ's message of redemption. It is in knowing the darkness of America's past that the light of biblical truth can shine more brightly.

It was under the ministry and teaching of Reverend Dr. William C. Turner Jr., a man who had lived through the Civil Rights struggles as a teenager, that I began to connect these historical truths with biblical revelation. Through his teaching and preaching, I came to see that slavery and its aftermath were not ancient relics, but living realities that continued to shape the moral and social fabric of this nation. Many of the events that defined the Civil Rights era occurred within a mere three decades of my own birth—barely a heartbeat in the measure of time. That realization deepened my awareness that America's original sins of slavery and racial hatred had not been buried with the past, but continued to live in the hearts of many.

Now, at the age of sixty, with greater understanding born of faith and years of reflection, I can say that the past truly does live in the future. The evils that were planted in the soil of this nation still yield fruit today. Yet, it is through the preaching of the Gospel that God continues to call His people toward repentance, reconciliation, and the healing of all brokenness. It is only in understanding what has been that we can discern what must be redeemed.

And so, as we turn now to the story of freedom rising in America—from the cries of the oppressed to the marches of the courageous—we do so with the awareness that history is not a closed book. It breathes, it bleeds, and it beckons every generation to confront its truths anew.

TONY L. SCOTT

The Groveland Four, Emmett Till, and the Moral Spark of a Movement, 1949-1955

The story of African American struggle in the mid-20th century begins with moments that pierced the conscience of a nation and laid bare the brutality and injustice embedded in American life. One of the earliest flashpoints in this period was the tragic case of the Groveland Four in 1949. Four young Black men in Lake County, Florida—***Earnest Thomas, Charles Greenlee, Samuel Shepherd,*** and ***Walter Irvin***—were falsely accused of raping a white woman.

Their ordeal exposed the lethal combination of racial prejudice, flawed law enforcement, and an indifferent judicial system. Because of racial hatred, Samuel Shepherd was killed by Sheriff McCall; however, Walter Irvin had survived the attempted murder of McCall, Ernest Thomas was killed by a white mob in 1949, and Charles Greenelee was imprisoned for life. He was a juvenile at the time and was later paroled. These men became emblematic of a system that sought to dehumanize Black bodies and deny justice, even when innocence was evident.

Just six years later, in 1955, the world was confronted with the brutal lynching of Emmett Till, a fourteen-year-old boy from Chicago visiting family in Mississippi. Till's murder—triggered by a false accusation and carried out with horrifying cruelty—was a clarion call for a generation that could no longer ignore the deadly consequences of racial hatred. Photographs of Till's mutilated body, published in newspapers and magazines across the country, shocked the conscience of the American public and galvanized a fledgling movement demanding justice. The Emmett Till case illustrated not only the physical danger faced by Black

Americans in the Jim Crow South but also the moral imperative for action, as silent complicity had long permitted such atrocities to flourish.

These slayings were interwoven with other horrors and critical moments that signaled both resistance and hope. The Montgomery Bus Boycott in 1955, sparked by the courageous defiance of Rosa Parks, demonstrated the power of collective action and the growing organizational capacity of the Black community. Ordinary men and women, working through churches, civic groups, and local leadership, began to understand that the struggle for equality required both persistence and strategic unity. The boycott was more than a protest—it was a declaration that African Americans would no longer tolerate a system designed to subjugate them.

The experiences of the Groveland Four, Emmett Till, and the Montgomery Bus Boycott were, in many ways, the sparks that ignited the broader Civil Rights Movement. These events revealed a nation grappling with its moral failures while simultaneously presenting opportunities for courage, resilience, and faith-driven activism. They illustrated the inextricable link between the personal and the political, showing that the fight for justice required both moral clarity and collective action.

As we reflect on these early flashpoints, it is essential to recognize that the sacrifices and courage of these individuals—and the countless unnamed others—created the foundation upon which future victories would be built. Their suffering, and the outrage it inspired, set the stage for the relentless push toward equality that would define the Civil Rights Era.

TONY L. SCOTT

The Little Rock Nine, Greensboro Sit-Ins, and Freedom Rides, 1957-1961

In 1957, the nation watched as nine African American students, later known as the Little Rock Nine, courageously entered Little Rock Central High School in Arkansas. This moment, coming three years after the Supreme Court's landmark decision in Brown v. Board of Education (1954) that declared segregation in public schools unconstitutional, revealed the deep resistance to integration in the South. The students faced relentless harassment, threats, and the physical presence of the Arkansas National Guard, deployed under Governor Orval Faubus's orders to block their entry. President Eisenhower intervened by sending federal troops to enforce the law, signaling that the federal government, though slow and hesitant, could be compelled to uphold justice. The bravery of these young students highlighted both the cruelty of entrenched racism and the extraordinary courage required to confront it.

Three years later, in 1960, a new form of protest emerged: the Greensboro Sit-Ins. Four Black college students from North Carolina Agricultural and Technical State University courageously sat at a segregated Woolworth's lunch counter, demanding service. Their peaceful sit-in sparked a wave of similar actions across the South, engaging students, clergy, and community members in a nonviolent strategy of resistance. These sit-ins demonstrated that ordinary acts of courage could disrupt the machinery of segregation, challenging societal norms and forcing communities to confront their moral failings.

The Freedom Rides of 1961 continued this momentum. Integrated groups of activists rode buses through the Deep South to challenge segregation in interstate travel and public facilities. The riders faced violent mobs, brutal beatings, and arrests—yet they persisted, demonstrating a remarkable commitment to justice. The Freedom Rides exposed the federal government's initial hesitancy and eventually compelled stronger enforcement of desegregation laws. Each rider, black and white, risked life and liberty to affirm the principle that justice and equality were nonnegotiable rights.

Taken together, the Little Rock Nine, the Greensboro Sit-Ins, and the Freedom Rides illustrate a period in which African Americans, guided by courage, faith, and strategic planning, steadily challenged systemic oppression. These actions exemplify the shift from localized resistance to coordinated national activism, laying critical groundwork for the larger victories and tragedies of the mid-1960s.

The March on Washington, 16th Street Baptist Church Bombing, and Montgomery Marches, 1963-1965

The year 1963 stands as a watershed in the Civil Rights Movement, a period marked by both profound hope and unspeakable tragedy. The March on Washington for Jobs and Freedom, held on August 28, 1963, brought over 250,000 Americans of all races to the nation's capital. It was here that Dr. Martin Luther King Jr. delivered his iconic "I Have a Dream" speech, envisioning a nation where justice and equality would transcend color lines. This march was not merely a demonstration; it was a moral declaration that freedom, dignity, and civil rights were inalienable for every American. The courage of those who participated underscored a collective determination to confront systemic oppression peacefully yet powerfully.

Yet, this same year also bore witness to one of the most heinous acts of racial terror: the 16th Street Baptist Church bombing in Birmingham, Alabama. Four young Black girls—***Addie Mae Collins, Cynthia Wesley, Carole Robertson, and Denise McNair***—lost their lives in an explosion orchestrated by white supremacists. This horrific act of violence against children, in a sacred house of worship, exposed the virulent hatred that still permeated segments of American society and intensified national outrage. The bombing became a rallying point for activists and underscored the urgent need for federal intervention to protect African American lives and enforce civil rights.

In 1965, the struggle for equality reached a pivotal climax with the Montgomery to Selma Marches, a series of protests aimed at securing voting rights for Black Americans in the South. These marches, particularly the events of **"Bloody Sunday" on March 7, 1965**, revealed the systemic resistance to enfranchisement, as peaceful marchers were brutally attacked by police forces with dogs, officers wielding batons and tear gas, and Blacks being assaulted with the powerful force of water from fire hoses. Yet, the courage of these marchers, coupled with national attention, pressured the federal government to act. Their resilience directly contributed to the passage of the Voting Rights Act of 1965, a landmark achievement in American history.

These events—simultaneously uplifting and devastating—illustrate the dual realities of the Civil Rights era: the extraordinary bravery of ordinary people and the persistent violence of those determined to maintain white supremacy. The victories, though significant, were forged through blood, sacrifice, and unyielding faith in the promise of justice.

The Assassinations of Malcolm X, Dr. King, and Nationwide Riots, 1965-1968

The mid-to-late 1960s were a period of both heightened hope and profound sorrow for African Americans. In 1965, the nation was shaken by the assassination of **Malcolm X**, a leader whose voice had fiercely advocated for Black empowerment, self-determination, and the uncompromising pursuit of justice. His death underscored the peril faced by those who dared challenge systemic oppression and highlighted the fractures within the struggle itself—between those who advocated nonviolent resistance and those who pushed for self-defense and radical action.

Three years later, in 1968, the assassination of ***Dr. Martin Luther King Jr.*** in Memphis, Tennessee, sent shockwaves across the country. Dr. King, a prophetic voice for nonviolence, unity, and the moral imperative of justice, had become the embodiment of the Civil Rights Movement. His death ignited grief, anger, and outrage, resulting in nationwide riots that reflected the simmering frustration and pent-up fury of communities long denied justice and equality. Cities from Washington, D.C., to Chicago, Detroit, and beyond witnessed unrest that was both a cry for redress and an expression of the moral and political failures of the nation.

The assassinations of Malcolm X and Dr. King, coupled with the violent eruptions across the country, revealed a bitter truth: the struggle for equality was not only a legal or political fight but also a profound moral and spiritual battle. The African American community endured loss and violence while simultaneously asserting its dignity and demanding recognition as full citizens of the United States. These events shaped a generation, hardening resolve while deepening the awareness that true justice requires continual vigilance and engagement.

Together, the Montgomery Boycott, Little Rock Nine, Greensboro Sit-Ins, Freedom Rides, March on Washington, 16th Street Baptist Church bombing, Montgomery Marches, and the assassinations of Malcolm X and Dr. King create a tapestry of courage, sacrifice, and moral clarity. They are enduring reminders that the road to civil rights was—and remains—paved with both hope and blood, and that the pursuit of justice is never without struggle.

Dr. Martin Luther King and Malcolm X: Revered and Feared Targets of Racial Supremacy

Dr. Martin Luther King, Jr. and Malcolm X had emerged as two of the most prominent leaders of the African American struggle for freedom and justice during the 1950s and 1960s. Their messages, though different in method and tone, both confronted the deep moral sickness of a nation that professed liberty while perpetuating racial bondage. King's dream and Malcolm's demand were two sides of the same moral coin — each calling America to repent of its hypocrisy and to fulfill its own creed that all men are created equal.

The reverence of these leaders among African Americans and allies was matched by the fear and hostility of white supremacists, segregationists, and even segments of the federal government. Their courage to speak truth to power placed them under constant scrutiny — not only from the public eye but from the state itself. Through the FBI's Counter-Intelligence Program, known as COINTELPRO, both Dr. King and

Malcolm X became targets of illegal surveillance, harassment, and psychological warfare. Their phones were tapped, their associates infiltrated, and their reputations attacked by a federal agency more concerned with preserving the racial order than protecting constitutional rights.

J. Edgar Hoover, who led the Bureau at the time, viewed Dr. King as *"the most dangerous Negro in America,"* not because of violence, but because of his moral influence — the power of his nonviolent message to stir the conscience of a divided nation. Likewise, Malcolm X, whose call for Black dignity and self-determination exposed the false peace of racial subjugation, was branded a threat to national stability. The government's internal memoranda went so far as to warn against *"the rise of a Black Messiah* who could unify and electrify the militant Black nationalist movement." Both King and Malcolm, in their own way, represented that potential — prophetic voices capable of awakening not only the Black community but also the moral consciousness of the nation itself.

This same undercurrent of fear — the dread of a "Black Messiah" who might expose and challenge America's racial sins while embodying her highest democratic ideals — would resurface decades later with the election of President Barack Obama; hence *The Obama Effect*. For some, his ascent symbolized the nation's progress toward racial reconciliation; for others, it reignited old insecurities — insecurities that would later find expression in *The Rise of Trumpism*, this racial undercurrent and movement shallowly buried beneath the surface. The symbolic power that King and Malcolm once carried in the streets of America now stood embodied within the Oval Office, not through revolution or protest, but through democratic election. Yet even this expression of progress became, for many, a catalyst of backlash, revealing how deeply the myth of white supremacy remains intertwined with the nation's identity and fear.

Other public figures, both Black and white, played critical roles in amplifying the fight against racial injustice. Their voices — in journalism, music, ministry, and the arts — helped sustain the movement's momentum even as the forces of repression sought to silence it. The civil rights struggle was not merely a political effort but a spiritual confrontation with evil, demanding both courage and faith from those who stood on the front lines.

Dr. King, Malcolm X, and these activists laid the foundational groundwork for significant milestones in African American history. Their sacrifices opened doors that laws alone could never unlock, forging pathways toward greater equality while exposing the moral contradictions at the heart of the American experiment.

The lives, sacrifices, and teachings of Dr. King and Malcolm X remain instructive today. Their struggles remind us that freedom is never granted by the oppressor but wrested from the grip of injustice through faith, perseverance, and truth. The surveillance that sought to silence them instead amplified their witness, proving that no government file can contain a God-ordained call for justice. Their voices still echo through time — not as relics of a bygone era, but as living testimonies that righteousness, once awakened, cannot be destroyed.

Christian Response

As we reflect on the lives and legacies of Dr. Martin Luther King Jr. and Malcolm X, we are reminded that the pursuit of justice is inseparable from the call of God on our lives. Scripture teaches us, **"Learn to do good; seek justice, correct oppression; bring justice to the fatherless, plead the widow's cause"** (Isaiah 1:17). The courage displayed by these leaders was not merely political—it was profoundly spiritual, rooted in the recognition that God's justice must prevail over human sin and corruption.

The sacrifices of those who stood against systemic oppression reveal that God equips His people to confront fear, intimidation, and violence when righteousness calls. Their lives challenge us to examine our own hearts: Are we willing to speak truth, advocate for the oppressed, and act boldly in the face of injustice? As Paul wrote, **"Do not be overcome by evil, but overcome evil with good"** (Romans 12:21).

God calls His Church to embody reconciliation and healing, understanding that the wounds of racial injustice are not only social and political but deeply spiritual. By studying the struggles of Dr. King, Malcolm X, and countless other advocates for justice, we learn that the path to true equality is walked through prayer, courage, moral clarity, and relentless pursuit of what is right.

Ultimately, the work of justice is not completed in our own power but through reliance on God, who transforms hearts, mends divisions, and calls all people to recognize the image of God in one another. Just as the Lord delivered His people from bondage in days of old, so must His people today stand unwavering against systemic injustice, bringing light where there is darkness and hope where there is despair.

CHAPTER 4

Growing Up Black in America, The Weight and the Witness of Survival

I was born in 1965, a year that marked the height of the Civil Rights Movement, three years before Dr. King's assassination, two years after President Kennedy's assassination and the month following Malcolm X's assassination. America at that time was a nation wrestling with its promises and its failures—a country in the midst of transformation, yet still tethered to its old racial order. For African Americans and Black boys in particular, these were volatile and uncertain times, filled with both the echoes of progress and the persistent shadows of oppression.

Though my mother carefully shielded me and my siblings from overt racism in our early years, the subtle currents of prejudice were always present. Covert forms of systemic racism shaped the boundaries of opportunity, influencing schools, neighborhoods, and public spaces. It was a landscape in which invisibility could feel safer than confrontation, yet awareness could not be fully postponed. Before I reached my teenage years, the realities of being Black in America began to press upon me with undeniable clarity. Oblivious to the fact, nonetheless, subtle slights, unspoken limitations, and social expectations became part of the rhythm of daily life.

These early experiences were not merely social—they were personal. The tension between what was promised and what was practiced planted a seed of understanding: the struggle of Black America was both visible and unseen, political and in your face, historical and present. My initial but limited exposure to stories of our past, whether through the glimpses of history I absorbed or the narratives of elders in my community, underscored that survival required both resilience and faith.

The foundation of my journey toward understanding *America's original sin* was being laid throughout my life, although I was unaware of this preparation. Growing up Black in America meant navigating two intertwined realities: one that demeaned, diminished, or discounted, and one that affirmed, nurtured, and encouraged through faith, family, and community. Schools, workplaces, and public spaces carried unseen barriers; yet the church, the home, and the bonds of kinship provided strength and grounding for many Blacks. Each day presented the dual challenge of survival and witness, of walking with dignity in a society designed to question your worth while holding fast to the assurance of God's vision for justice.

In this chapter, we explore not just the hardships but the endurance, the strategic navigation, and the spiritual inheritance that shaped young African Americans like myself.

The Welfare State and the Wounding of the Black Family

As the civil rights movement subtly faded into memory and the hard realities of post-segregation America took hold, a new form of control emerged — one clothed not in chains, but in checks. The welfare state, introduced under the guise of compassion, promised relief to the poor and assistance to struggling families. Yet for countless Black households, unlike many white families who did in fact benefit from government assistance — asset building, this "help" for Black households came with hidden terms — restrictions that fractured homes, once again, displaced fathers, and redefined manhood in ways that would scar generations to come. And so it was, Blacks were provided assistance for survival, while white families were provided assistance for asset building.

To qualify for government aid, the Black mother often had to stand alone. The system demanded proof of poverty, and the presence of a working man in the home could disqualify the family from receiving assistance. In other words, for a mother to feed her children, she had to literally and figuratively push their father out, although many subverted the systems that fought against the family. Welfare caseworkers and social service agents would make unannounced visits, searching for evidence of a man's presence — a pair of men's shoes by the door, a razor on the bathroom sink, or the faint trace of cologne in the air. If found, benefits could be revoked. Poverty became policed, and the home — once sacred — became an inspected zone.

This was not simply a bureaucratic oversight. It was social engineering. Whether through ignorance or intent, these policies functioned as quiet weapons against Black stability. Some may argue that the architects of welfare meant well, that they sought only to lift the poor. But history teaches us that ignorance often serves as the mask of strategy. White fear of Black advancement was deeply rooted in the American imagination. The sight of a self-sufficient Black man — providing for his household, leading his family, and shaping his community — represented a threat to the social order white America had built. To diminish his role was to preserve control.

Thus, welfare for countless Blacks became a new plantation — one where dependence replaced whips, and policy replaced overseers. By rewarding absence and penalizing presence, the state or system, yet again, disrupted God's ordained design for the home. What centuries of bondage and Jim Crow could not fully erase, the welfare system eroded systematically, one father, one family at a time.

While white families were building generational wealth through access to suburban housing, federal programs, bank loans, college education, and preferential access to better jobs, Black families were redlined into dependency through discriminatory policies and practices. Segregation was no longer enforced by "Whites Only" signs but by zip codes, income brackets, and bureaucratic rules. The hand that offered *help* was also the hand that set the limits.

The effects were both economic and social. A people once bound together by faith, family, and resilience were now being reshaped by scarcity and state oversight. The erosion of the Black family left not just social but moral and emotional voids — children growing up without the daily guidance of their fathers, mothers bearing impossible burdens, and communities stripped of their central pillar of strength.

And yet, throughout all this, there remained a steadfast hope. A generation learned to survive not just the wounds of poverty but the wounds of policy. In the midst of broken systems, the image of God within the Black life of many refused to be erased. The struggle for dignity became a witness — a living testimony to the fact that no system, no matter how calculated, could completely destroy what God had ordained.

For many who grew up under these conditions, the struggle was not theoretical — it was personal. The realities of welfare dependency, racial discrimination, and economic exclusion were felt in daily life, shaping identity and faith alike. And it is from within that lived experience — from the weight and witness of survival — that aspects of my own story I now share.

The Thirst that Could Not Be Quenched

Let me now move forward about three years from another experience that I will share next. I, too, would come to know the sting of being denied, not by law, but by the lingering spirit of racism that refused to die. I was perhaps twelve or thirteen years old when I took on a small job selling newspapers at the intersection of Geer Street and Avondale Drive, located in Durham, my place of birth. It was honest work, and under the heat of the afternoon sun, I had earned a few dollars of my own.

At that same corner stood a small storefront, the kind that sold snacks and drinks to those passing by. I remember it clearly, though time has changed its appearance. The building that once held that store is now a Black-owned business where vehicle windows are tinted — a small symbol, perhaps, of how time can redeem what once wounded.

But that day, the memory was far from redemptive. Tired and thirsty, I stepped inside the store to buy a cold beverage. Seated within were four or five white men, their gazes fixed on me as I entered. Their eyes carried no warmth, only the quiet questioning of my presence — why are you here? What do you want?

Still, I approached respectfully and asked, "Can I buy something to drink?"

One of the men looked at me, half-smirking, and replied with mocking inflection, "Can you?"

The words hung in the air like smoke. There was faint laughter, a low ripple of amusement at my expense. I remember standing there, confused and uneasy. I didn't fully understand the meaning of the exchange, but I knew enough to feel its cruelty. The laughter was light, but the weight it carried was heavy.

So, I turned and walked away — my thirst unquenched, my dignity quietly bruised. It was not the kind of terror that shouts, but the kind that whispers, that seeps into the conscience and lingers for years.

Looking back, I see now what I could not then: that racism wears many faces. Sometimes it marches in mobs and burns crosses; other times, it sits comfortably in chairs and mocks a child's right to be human. It is the same spirit, merely dressed in different garments.

That moment, simple as it may seem, taught me something profound about America — that the wound of racism was not only in its violence, but also in its everydayness. It was in the smirk, the question, the denied drink, the feeling that you didn't belong. Those moments may not make the headlines, but they make the man.

Playing While Black

As a child of around nine years old, attending Merrick-Moore Elementary School—named after two prominent Black men—I experienced one of my earliest lessons in the harsh realities of racial prejudice. My friend and I had wandered behind a local business, Canada Dry, located on Hardee Street; this was not far from where I lived, Cheek Road Apartments, Apt. 11-B. Behind the building were stacks of wooden pallets forming a makeshift mountain that drew the curiosity of any young boy. What we saw as adventure, the white world saw as trespass. Either someone called the police, or a white officer on patrol noticed us; in short order, we were placed in the back of a patrol car. When another officer arrived and inquired about our presence, the first officer's words cut deep: "I have two niggers on the property." I was too young to fully comprehend the systemic cruelty in that statement, yet I knew instinctively that something was profoundly wrong.

Not long after, I faced another act of everyday injustice. Riding my bicycle to Ken's Quickie Mart, located at Hardee Street and Cheek Road, my handlebars lightly brushed a store window—an accident of childhood. Yet the white clerk, seething with disdain, threatened to throw my bicycle into a trash can. I scoffed at his words. I responded, "Know you won't," only to witness him act upon them. Shocked, I returned home to recount the incident. When my dad returned home, my mother informed my father, who then went to confront the man. In fear of reprisal from my dad, a mentally and physically strong Black man, the clerk locked himself inside the cooler, revealing the tension, fear, and power imbalance inherent in such a potentially volatile encounter when a father, a Black man, is in his rightful place to defend his family.

Around the same period, my father himself experienced unjust treatment at the hands of law enforcement. While driving his vehicle without shoes, a white officer stopped him and subjected him to unwarranted harassment. Even something as minor as bare feet became a pretext for intimidation—a stark reminder that systemic racism did not spare even the simplest of actions.

Now, at the age of thirteen or fourteen, my friend Bryant Cates and I experienced yet another form of racism while riding our bicycles down Club Boulevard near Roxboro Street. Two white men, likely in their late teens or early twenties, shouted a derisive comment: "Snowballs! Who shitted on you?" The language was crude and dehumanizing, and though I did not fully comprehend it at the time, its intent later became clear. Such encounters taught that even ordinary acts of childhood play could be perceived as a challenge to racial hierarchies, subjecting Black children to scrutiny, mockery, and intimidation.

These experiences, though formative and relatively minor in their physical consequences, underscore a larger and more insidious reality: the pervasive surveillance and policing of Black bodies, even in acts as innocent as play. The policing of our movements, the casual cruelty of adults, and the omnipresent threat of law enforcement foreshadowed the dangers that have tragically claimed the lives of countless Black children throughout history—children like **Emmett Till**, whose life and brutal death remain a grim testament to racial hatred and violence.

From Canada Dry to Club Boulevard, from my own encounters to those endured by my father and other Black adults, the pattern was clear: a society that normalized suspicion, indignity, and oppression against its Black citizens. These were not isolated incidents; they were lived expressions of systemic injustice. And while my friend and I escaped physical harm, the memory of those encounters, the humiliation and fear, left a lasting imprint—an early lesson in the resilience required to survive as Black in America.

Experiences of Racism in Young Adulthood

Even as I moved from the innocence of childhood into young adulthood, the shadows of racism remained, though often cloaked in subtler, insidious forms. By the summer of 1983, I had enlisted in the United States Army, seeking both personal growth and a way to serve my country. Yet, even in uniform, the biases of others sought to define me. A white basic training drill sergeant, SSgt. Grimm singled me out for reasons I could not comprehend at the time. Observing the confidence I carried within myself, he perceived a threat to his white authority. In front of my peers, he asked where I was from—assuming that someone with my self-assurance must have migrated to the North with my family, and therefore I was viewed as a Northerner. He said as much. When I said Durham, North Carolina, the implication was clear: I was not supposed to possess such confidence as a Southern Black man.

Unbeknownst to him, my preparation—physical and mental—had equipped me to meet the demands of basic training. I had trained diligently, and my competence became undeniable. I was promoted to squad leader and later to platoon guide, roles that demanded leadership and responsibility. A Black drill sergeant, Staff Sergeant Dorsey, recognized my capabilities and affirmed my potential. Yet when he took leave due to family bereavement, the white drill sergeant, along with other soldiers in training, conspired to undermine my position, attempting to strip me of the authority I had earned. This was not an isolated incident. The persistence of racial prejudice in the Army revealed itself repeatedly, a constant reminder that merit alone did not shield one from the corrosive effects of systemic racism.

Even after my honorable discharge, the patterns followed me. When I became a Durham police officer, I encountered a microcosm of the same biases I had seen in the military. Though I will not go into details in this book, I explore both my Army and Durham Police Department experiences in greater detail in my other work, **Sentinel of Service: Protecting Durham**, *the Bull City, with the subtitle Policing's Evolution Nationally and Locally, Preserving the Legacy of the Historic Hayti District.* These stories demonstrate the lived reality of being a Black male navigating institutions that sought to test, limit, and control, rather than recognize competence or humanity.

Through all of these challenges, each encounter—whether in childhood, in military training, or in law enforcement—reinforced the stark reality of racial prejudice and the resilience required to navigate a society that sought to define and limit you. These lived experiences—the childhood encounters, the confrontations with authority in youth, and the professional challenges as an adult—illustrate the enduring weight and witness of survival as a Black male in America. They are part of a larger narrative, one that is both deeply personal and historically rooted, revealing the persistent forces that shape the Black experience and the strength required to navigate them.

As I near the close of this chapter, I am confident in saying that every Black male of my generation—and certainly those who came before me—can share their stories, their lived experiences, and those of others, of encountering racism while playing, learning, and maturing in America. This is a sad commentary, but it is a story that needs to be told and heard, particularly by whites, so that understanding, reconciliation, and healing can begin, and unity within this divided nation may be sought.

Even so, moving beyond my personal experiences as a child, teenager, and young adult, I, as a father, had to confront racism in order to safeguard my own children. One such encounter occurred when my youngest son, Desmond, was attending Merrick Moore Elementary School. At the time, I was a plainclothes law enforcement detective, well respected within my community.

On this particular day, I visited the school during the annual end-of-year field day. As I approached my son, I noticed concern on his face. Something had transpired, and I needed to understand it. Because I had always instilled in him the importance of respecting authority and maintaining proper behavior, Desmond initially believed that the correction he had received from the school principal, Mr. Rigdon (also my former principal), was justified. My son explained that Mr. Rigdon had grabbed his shoulder/arm in a manner that I found entirely unacceptable.

I approached Mr. Rigdon respectfully but firmly, stating that his actions were unacceptable and that he was never to put his hands on my son again.

I spoke without wavering, unapologetically, and he knew I meant every word. Mr. Rigdon then threatened to report me to my superiors because of the way I, as a mentally and physically strong Black father, had asserted myself. I told him, "Do what you think you need to do," but he understood the conviction behind my words – don't put your hands on my son again.

Interestingly, this encounter echoed a story my mother had shared after the fact, about her own confrontation with Mr. Rigdon decades earlier. When my younger sister and I both attended Merrick Moore, he had threatened her physically, saying he would "smack her face." My mother confronted him immediately, declaring that he would not lay hands on her daughter. And so, like my mother and father, I, too, as a strong Black man, stood firmly in defense of my child.

I did so without regret, and I remain committed to standing as a strong, godly, Christian Black man. Such men are needed today—not just for the protection of their children, but as pillars in the ongoing fight against the false and destructive ideology of white supremacy. And equally, strong, godly, Christian white men are needed today as allies in this struggle, so that together we may confront and dismantle the enduring legacy of racial oppression.

Christian Response

In every age and under every system of oppression, there have been those who carried the scars of injustice upon their bodies and their souls. The story of the Black experience in America—marked by struggle, by endurance, and by the will to survive—is not merely sociological; it is deeply spiritual. It mirrors the ancient cry of God's people under Pharaoh's lash, of exiles by the rivers of Babylon, and of disciples walking with their risen Lord through a world that still crucifies innocence.

When we consider the weight of racism, we must remember that sin, in all its forms, is rebellion against God's order. Racism is not merely prejudice—it is pride deified. It is the elevation of self and skin above the Creator who **"hath made of one blood all nations of men for to dwell on all the face of the earth"** (Acts 17:26). It is, therefore, not just a social sickness but a spiritual warfare—a battle between light and darkness, truth and deception, humility and arrogance.

And yet, the same God who heard the groanings of His people in Egypt is the same God who sees the afflictions of those oppressed by the hand of racial hatred. He is the God who still declares, **"I have surely seen the affliction of my people which are in Egypt, and have heard their cry by reason of their taskmasters; for I know their sorrows"** (Exodus 3:7). The Lord not only sees—He intervenes. He raises up deliverers, He equips voices, and He strengthens those who stand for righteousness even when misunderstood or maligned.

My experiences—as a child bewildered by hate, as a soldier confronting discrimination, as a father protecting his son—speak to the generational persistence of evil and yet the greater persistence of grace. These are not stories of bitterness, but of awareness. Not tales of despair, but of discernment. Through them, we see that even when the structures of man fail, the sovereignty of God prevails.

For it is written: **"The Lord executeth righteousness and judgment for all that are oppressed"** (Psalm 103:6). The believer's response, therefore, must not be retaliation but revelation—the revelation of Christ's love that disarms the hatred of this world. The child of God must never forget that **"vengeance belongs to the Lord"** and that *justice delayed is never justice denied* when placed into His eternal hands.

Racism, though systemic and ancient, will one day meet its end. Every false ideology, every proud heart, and every oppressive system will bow before the King of Glory. For Scripture assures us that in that great multitude before the throne, all nations, kindreds, people, and tongues shall stand clothed in white robes, crying with one voice, **"Salvation to our God which sitteth upon the throne, and unto the Lamb"** (Revelation 7:9–10). In that day, there will be no more dividing lines, no more color-coded hierarchies, no more supremacy of man—but only the supremacy of Christ.

Until that day, we who walk by faith **must do justice, love mercy, and walk humbly with our God** (Micah 6:8). We must expose darkness by living as children of light. And when we stand, as I once stood, and continue to stand before the powers that be—whether in schools, in streets, or in systems—we must speak truth without trembling, love without compromising, and forgive without forgetting the lessons learned.

This is not weakness; it is divine strength. For Christ Himself, when reviled, reviled not again, but committed Himself to Him who judges righteously. And it is in this same spirit that we labor, suffer, and stand—knowing that **"the sufferings of this present time are not worthy to be compared with the glory which shall be revealed in us"** (Romans 8:18).

So then, let every reader take heed. The struggle against racism is not only America's unfinished business—it is the Church's unfinished calling. The answer has never been in politics or protest alone, but in repentance, reconciliation, and renewal through Jesus Christ our Lord. For only when hearts are changed by His indwelling Spirit will the land be healed by His grace.

CHAPTER 5

The Trumps: Father, Son, and the Systems - A Legacy of American Racism

Fred Trump: The Patriarch and the Pattern

Nothing happens in a vacuum.

To understand the world Donald Trump inherited—and the racial lens through which he would later view it—we must first examine the man who shaped him: Fred Trump, father, real estate magnate, and a figure whose life and actions no doubt left an indelible imprint on his son… like father, like son. Fred Trump's record is a study in contrasts: a businessman celebrated for his acumen, yet also a man whose practices reinforced racial hierarchies, both intentionally and through the exploitations of a racially biased system.

Fred Trump's involvement with racialized practices was not incidental. His name appears in public records connected to a KKK rally (May 31, 1927), reflecting at minimum an alignment or one can argue a curiosity with a culture of racial terror. More systematically, he was repeatedly sued for violating the Fair Housing Act, accused of using racial slurs, and cited for housing code violations—an environment in which Black tenants were denied basic access to housing, stability, and economic opportunity. These events were not isolated missteps; they were the markers of a broader, sustained pattern of racial exclusion and discrimination.

Operating in New York City, a northern urban center often imagined as more progressive than the South, Fred Trump leveraged the tools of systemic racism with calculated precision. Redlining, restrictive covenants, and discriminatory tenant selection were not abstract policy terms—they were mechanisms Fred Trump employed to maintain control, maximize profit, and cement a social hierarchy through which he attempted to exclude African Americans from both the neighborhoods and the wealth he cultivated. In doing so, he contributed directly to the economic oppression and housing segregation that would plague generations of Black families.

For a young Donald Trump, growing up in this environment, the lessons were vivid. He observed a father who could assert power, manipulate systems, evade accountability, and profit within a racially stratified society. The implicit moral calculus was clear: self-interest, boldness, and strategic audacity were rewarded; empathy and consideration for the oppressed were optional. These were formative experiences that one can reason, shaped his understanding of authority, influence, and the means by which advantage could be preserved.

Fred Trump's actions reveal a continuity between personal bias and structural inequity. Individual prejudice, when enacted through wealth, power, and societal structures, has consequences that ripple across generations. Black Americans, denied housing and economic mobility, faced barriers to wealth accumulation, community stability, and intergenerational progress. The pattern established by Fred Trump illuminates how systemic inequities are reinforced and reproduced—not by accident, but by deliberate actions, choices, and the modeling of behavior for the next generation.

In understanding Fred Trump, we see both the man and the system, the personal and the structural. This is essential because the lessons Donald Trump absorbed in youth—about power, social positioning, and race— would later influence his worldview, policies, and public actions. The patriarch's influence created a pattern, one in which the pursuit of self-interest could overshadow the moral and social consequences of maintaining racial hierarchies.

Donald Trump: The Inheritance of Racism

Donald Trump's formative years unfolded against the turbulent backdrop of the Civil Rights era, a period that reshaped the nation's moral and social landscape but left indelible marks on individuals and families alike. Born into a household shaped by his father, Fred Trump, Donald's understanding of race, power, and privilege was neither abstract nor accidental; it was inherited, observed, and reinforced within the walls of his home and the streets of Queens, New York.

As a young man, Donald did not witness the assassinations of President John F. Kennedy in 1963 or Dr. Martin Luther King Jr. in 1968 firsthand. Nevertheless, through the media outlets of the time and the conversations within his sphere of influence, he had to have become keenly aware of these national tragedies. He was seventeen when Kennedy was killed, and twenty-one at the time of King's assassination. These events, widely reported and discussed, I would imagine left an impression on young

Donald, shaping his perception of societal upheaval, race relations, and the necessity of defending one's familial and economic position in a world of uncertainty. Guided by the perspectives of his father and those likeminded with Fred Trump, these events had to have — reason suggests as much, reinforced an understanding of race and privilege as inseparable from power and influence.

Fred Trump, already a dominant figure in real estate and construction in Queens, exemplified this defense of status. His actions and attitudes toward Black Americans reflected both personal prejudice and the broader systemic racism of mid-twentieth-century urban America. With Fred's history involving racially charged events, his arrest at the KKK rally, repeated accusations of racial discrimination in housing, and civil suits under the Fair Housing Act. These experiences were not mere footnotes; they established patterns of thought and behavior, demonstrating to his son the ways in which power, property, and race intersected in practical and often oppressive ways.

From the beginning, Donald's worldview was shaped not only by observing his father navigate—and at times manipulate—the racial and legal structures around him, but also by the voices, counsel, and actions of others in his circle who shared Fred Trump's perspectives. The practices Fred employed, whether consciously exploitative or reflective of widespread societal norms, conveyed clear lessons: the economic and social elevation of white families could be maintained by controlling who gained access to homes, neighborhoods, and opportunity. Donald inherited not just wealth, but a template for understanding the nation's racial hierarchy, the mechanisms of exclusion, and strategies for preserving privilege.

It is crucial to recognize that nothing in this narrative of written and unwritten history occurs in a vacuum. The lessons Donald absorbed were reinforced by the neighborhoods he lived in, the schools he attended, and the communities in which he moved. There is always cause and effect. The experiences of his father, the segregated conditions of New York City housing, and the responses to the Civil Rights Movement all shaped a young man whose perception of race and power would later influence the highest offices in the United States.

Fred Trump's influence on Donald had to be profound (like father, like son), but it was likely neither solely instructive nor overt. Rather, it was the daily observation of authority, entitlement, and selective adherence to law that cemented a worldview: the benefits of systemic power could be claimed, wielded, and preserved, often at the expense of others, particularly Black Americans seeking equality. In this way, Donald Trump's early life reflected the continuity of racial inequities, inherited patterns, and the subtle yet potent ways in which familial example merges with societal structure to reproduce advantage and exclusion.

The inheritance of racism was not limited to overt acts or public controversies. It was encoded in the culture of expectation, in spoken norms as well as unspoken norms, and in neighborhood dynamics. I am convinced that the young Donald learned, observed, and internalized these lessons, setting the stage for the later actions, rhetoric, and policies that would define his public life. As we consider his ascent and broader influence—Trumpism, it becomes clear: the past is always living in the future. What was learned in the home, witnessed in the streets, absorbed from others who shared his father's views, and reinforced by the media of the day would echo in the decisions, statements, and governance of his later years.

The Intergenerational Logic of White Supremacy

The legacy of white supremacy is neither accidental nor sporadic. It is a careful, deliberate system of thought and behavior, preached in many white evangelical churches, taught in Sunday school classes, discussed amongst the think-tanks of white elites, and passed from one generation to the next. This inheritance shapes not only social norms and institutional policies but also personal attitudes, family values, and the very imagination of what is possible for those deemed "other." It is a logic that whispers, often unspoken yet profoundly felt, in boardrooms, on streets, and in the private conversations of those who hold privilege.

From the patterns observed in the lives of men like Fred Trump, the patriarch, it becomes clear that these lessons were imparted intentionally. The lessons of racial hierarchy, social dominance, and fear of Black advancement were modeled in family behaviors, business dealings, and social associations. Children who grew up in these environments absorbed a worldview in which power, wealth, and whiteness were inextricably linked. The next generation—Donald Trump, in this case—did not inherit just property or opportunity but also a blueprint for how to navigate and exploit systems of privilege while remaining insulated from the consequences often faced by marginalized communities.

The intergenerational logic is evident in both subtle and explicit forms. It manifests in private conversations about "neighborhoods," in coded language about who belongs, and in strategic decisions that affect the lives of those outside the sphere of privilege. This logic is not merely anecdotal; it is institutionalized, embedded in economic practices, housing policies, and social hierarchies that continue to shape American life. Under Donald Trump's second term as the president of the United States, we are witnessing this harsh reality emerge boldly once again.

It is imperative to recognize that the inheritance of white supremacy is not limited to one family or one locality—it is national, systemic, and ongoing. The structures that sustain it are reinforced by socialization, law, and the tacit consent of those who benefit from it. Leadership, moral authority, and platforms of influence must confront this reality directly. Injustice and lawlessness must be called out wherever they appear, and accountability must not be selective. Those in power, regardless of office or influence, cannot be given a pass.

The consequences of neglecting this moral imperative are clear, but this also should be the case wherever injustice, lawlessness, and immorality arise to negatively impact a society. In this matter before you, without vigilance, the intergenerational patterns of white supremacy continue, shaping public policy, public sentiment, and public leadership in ways that perpetuate inequality and undermine the promise of justice. Understanding this ungodly inheritance of pride and hierarchy is essential, for only by recognizing the deliberate and systemic nature of these forces can society begin to dismantle them.

Redlining and Economic Oppression

As previously pointed out, redlining was more than an economic policy—it was a deliberate, systemic tool of racial control that shaped the destiny of Black communities across America. Maps drawn by federal agencies and banks in the 1930s designated Black neighborhoods as "high risk" for mortgages, effectively cutting off access to homeownership, capital investment, and the foundation for generational wealth. These neighborhoods were outlined in red, a stark signal that opportunity and prosperity were to be withheld. The message was clear: Black lives and Black communities were considered expendable in the pursuit of white economic security.

The consequences for Black families were immediate and enduring. Without access to mortgages, property values in Black neighborhoods stagnated, schools were underfunded, streets and infrastructure decayed, and local businesses struggled to survive. Even those who managed to buy homes faced predatory lending and discriminatory practices designed to strip them of any wealth they might accrue. Redlining was not simply an economic decision—it was a social weapon, a method to contain and suppress Black life while allowing white families to flourish.

By mid-century, traditional methods of displacement compounded these injustices. Urban renewal projects, often cloaked in the language of progress, destroyed long-established Black neighborhoods in cities like Durham, North Carolina, my hometown and place of birth, as well as New Haven, Connecticut; Richmond, Virginia; St. Louis, Missouri; and others. Entire communities were razed to make way for highways, industrial zones, or luxury housing for white residents. In Durham, the historic Hayti District, once known as Black Wall Street, thrived as a center of Black entrepreneurship, culture, and community. Yet in the 1960s and 1970s, urban renewal policies and the construction of a highway (NC 147) literally cut through this neighborhood, displacing families, closing businesses, and erasing a vibrant cultural and economic hub.

The process of gentrification is the modern continuation of this systemic displacement. In Durham, and in many other historically Black cities, longtime residents now struggle not only to buy homes in the neighborhoods where they were raised but also to remain in them. Rising property values, increased property taxes, and the influx of new, wealthier residents create barriers that make it nearly impossible for many Black families to stay. What was once revitalization is, in effect, a new wave of economic exclusion—progress achieved at the expense of those who built these communities.

The long-term impact of these policies is unmistakable. Generational wealth for Black families was systematically denied, the racial wealth gap widened, and social mobility remained out of reach for millions. The psychological toll was also profound, as families internalized the message that opportunity was not meant for them, no matter how hard they worked or how faithfully they contributed to their communities.

Redlining, urban renewal, and gentrification illustrate a sobering principle: nothing happens in a vacuum. Decisions made decades ago continue to shape housing, education, and economic opportunity today. Without vigilance, the patterns established by these systems continue to marginalize Black communities, perpetuate inequality, and undermine justice. Urban planning, gentrification, and economic "progress" cannot be divorced from their historical context; the erasure of Black neighborhoods under the guise of development is both a continuation of systemic oppression and a moral failing of society at large.

The story of redlining, urban renewal, and gentrification is a cautionary tale: the structures of oppression are deliberate, and the consequences—economic, social, and cultural—are profound and enduring. Recognizing this is essential if the promise of equity and justice is to be pursued, and if the voices of communities that were displaced, flooded, or erased are to be heard and honored.

The Racial Wealth Gap and Housing Discrimination

These matters must be underscored:

The economic inequalities that Black Americans faced and experience today are neither accidental nor abstract—they are the cumulative result of centuries of exclusion, discrimination, and policy-driven barriers. And so it was, redlining established the initial framework by which Black families were systematically denied access to homeownership and wealth-building opportunities. This initial exclusion, however, was only the starting point of a much broader and persistent racial wealth gap.

Then there was housing discrimination that extended beyond the denial of mortgages. Black families often faced predatory lending, inflated interest rates, and restrictive covenants that barred them from moving into predominantly "white neighborhoods." Even when legal avenues opened in theory—through the Fair Housing Act of 1968—the enforcement was uneven, and discrimination persisted in subtler, yet equally destructive, forms. Real estate agents steered Black homebuyers toward less desirable areas, landlords imposed onerous restrictions, and zoning laws were applied in ways that reinforced segregation.

The consequences of this discrimination were profound and generational. Wealth, built primarily through home equity, became concentrated within white families, while Black families were consistently denied the opportunity not only to accumulate but also to transfer property-based wealth to future generations. The disparities are striking: Black households today hold a fraction of the wealth of their white counterparts, with homeownership still a primary determinant of financial stability, social mobility, and access to quality education.

In my city of Durham, gentrification intensifies this dynamic. Historically Black neighborhoods, like the old Hayti District, are at this very moment facing skyrocketing property values, forcing longtime residents out of communities their families built over decades. While labeled "revitalization" or "progress," these developments primarily benefit outside investors and new, predominantly white residents, further widening the racial wealth gap. So, it is a fact that the structural barriers that began with redlining are reinforced by modern economic pressures, keeping Black families from reclaiming ground lost through decades of systemic discrimination.

The racial wealth gap is not limited to housing alone. Access to capital, employment opportunities, and educational resources are all intertwined, creating a cycle where economic inequality begets social inequality, which then perpetuates further economic disparity. It is a stark reminder that nothing happens in a vacuum: the historical policies of exclusion directly inform the inequities experienced by Black Americans today.

Recognizing the structural and intentional nature of these barriers is essential; enough can not be stated regarding these matters. Without deliberate policy interventions and societal accountability, these patterns will persist, denying equity and opportunity to generations yet to come. Housing discrimination, intertwined with wealth inequality, is both a symptom and a perpetuator of systemic oppression—a legacy that continues to demand attention, understanding, and action.

These entrenched inequities, as mentioned, do not exist in isolation—nothing happens in a vacuum, cause and effect are always married together, bringing advantage to some and leaving others behind. They are part of a continuum of systemic barriers that constrain the possibilities of Black communities, shaping the environment in which young people grow, learn, and are expected to thrive.

It is within this context that many Black children find themselves at the intersection of underfunded schools, over-policed neighborhoods, and limited economic mobility—a convergence that feeds directly into what has come to be known as the school-to-prison pipeline. There is always cause and effect: generations of structural disadvantage, reinforced by discriminatory policies, produce measurable consequences for communities. As we move into the next section, it becomes clear that these structural injustices are not simply historical artifacts; the past is always living in the future, continuing to shape the futures of generations yet to come.

School-to-Prison Pipeline, Historical Roots, and Modern Realities

The school-to-prison pipeline is not a sudden or isolated phenomenon. It is a structural and historical continuity, an outgrowth of systemic oppression that has been embedded in the DNA of America since the 17th century. Its maturation can be traced to the 13th Amendment, which, while abolishing slavery, included a critical loophole: "except as a punishment for crime whereof the party shall have been duly convicted."

This clause allowed a new form of forced labor (convict leasing) to take hold, targeting Black communities under the guise of criminal justice. Prisons became extensions of the labor system that slavery had established, with Black bodies subjected to control, exploitation, and marginalization under a legal framework that perpetuated inequality.

Over the decades, the rise of prison labor and the growth of the carceral state became deeply entwined with economic exploitation that further benefited whites. Black men and women, disproportionately criminalized and incarcerated, were channeled into labor programs within the prison system that often mirrored the conditions of antebellum servitude. In this historical continuity, we see clearly that nothing happens in a vacuum; the legacies of slavery and Jim Crow continue to echo through modern policies, shaping both opportunity and limitation for Black communities.

Schools, far from being neutral spaces of learning, have historically reflected these broader societal inequities. Underfunding of Black schools intersects with disciplinary policies that criminalize normal childhood behavior. Zero-tolerance policies, harsh suspensions, and expulsions disproportionately target Black students, pushing them into contact with the juvenile and criminal justice systems at an early age. In many ways, schools have become the entry points into the same structures that perpetuate economic and social marginalization, continuing the intergenerational patterns of oppression we have traced thus far.

The War on Drugs

The War on Drugs, particularly in the 1980s and 1990s, further intensified the pipeline. Policies that ostensibly addressed crime disproportionately targeted Black neighborhoods, criminalizing poverty and survival behaviors while leaving white communities largely untouched. Mandatory minimum sentencing, aggressive prosecutorial practices, and laws such as the "three strikes" rule ensured that individuals, Blacks specifically, could receive disproportionately long sentences for non-violent offenses. Here, and yet again, we witness cause and effect: laws and policies, shaped by systemic bias and fear, directly affected the opportunities, futures, and freedoms of entire generations.

Once a person has been convicted of a felony, the repercussions extend far beyond prison walls. Felon disenfranchisement restricts the right to vote, limits access to employment, housing, and education, and places barriers to economic advancement. The social stigma attached to a criminal record compounds these structural inequities, reducing the ability of individuals to rebuild their lives and contribute meaningfully to their communities. In this way, incarceration and sentencing policies, while ostensibly about justice, perpetuate generational cycles of poverty, marginalization, and racial inequality.

The consequences of this system are stark. Entire communities have been destabilized, families fractured, and the prospects of economic advancement curtailed. Yet, the pipeline is not merely the result of one law, one policy, or one generation of lawmakers; it is the product of a historical continuum in which the past is always living in the future. From the 13th Amendment to modern carceral practices, we see the deliberate shaping of society to marginalize, punish, and control Black populations. Schools and prisons, though ostensibly separate institutions, operate in tandem to reinforce these patterns.

It is also critical to recognize the human cost of this pipeline. Black children, removed from educational opportunities, subjected to criminalization, and socialized into environments of fear and suspicion, experience lifelong consequences. Communities bear the burden of systemic neglect, as talent, energy, and cultural capital are siphoned off into a system designed not to cultivate, but to contain and control. As I have noted earlier in this chapter, gentrification, economic oppression, and the intergenerational logic of white supremacy compound these harms, creating layered and enduring challenges for Black Americans.

The school-to-prison pipeline, then, is neither accidental nor inevitable. It is a continuation of historical practices, policies, and norms that, without vigilance, persist and evolve. As with all systemic injustices, it demands both recognition and accountability. Leadership, community engagement, and policy reform must confront these realities directly; no institution or actor can remain passive. And in this case, without vigilance, the intergenerational patterns of white supremacy continue, shaping public policy, public sentiment, and public leadership in ways that perpetuate inequality and undermine the promise of justice.

I close this chapter with the reminder that the consequences of neglecting this moral imperative are clear—but this also must be the case wherever injustice, lawlessness, and immorality arise to negatively impact a society. The school-to-prison pipeline, the legacy of the 13th Amendment, the rise of prison labor, the War on Drugs, and discriminatory sentencing practices are all part of a larger, persistent system of oppression that demands our understanding, our attention, and our action.

TONY L. SCOTT

Overcoming Racial Trauma Through Faith and Resilience

And so it is, the experience of racism is neither abstract nor isolated; it is lived daily by Black Americans, adults and youth alike. These encounters, whether subtle microaggressions or overt acts of discrimination, accumulate over time, leaving deep emotional, psychological, and spiritual scars. Racial trauma is real, persistent, and pervasive, but it is not the only source of suffering. Individuals and communities face a wide range of hardships—poverty, violence, neglect, and systemic inequities—that compound the weight of lived experiences.

For many, faith becomes both anchor and compass amid these realities. Faith does not erase trauma or hardship; rather, it offers a framework for resilience, perspective, and moral clarity. It allows individuals to name the harm, grieve, and pursue restoration while maintaining hope and agency in the face of adversity. Historically, the Black church has served as sanctuary and catalyst for empowerment, guiding generations to navigate oppression with courage and dignity.

Yet not everyone possesses a foundation of faith or a support system. Those without these anchors are particularly vulnerable. The inevitable consequence of prolonged exposure to trauma—whether racial, social, or economic—is a sense of helplessness and hopelessness. When left unchecked, the rage and frustration born from such circumstances often manifest in destructive behaviors, both individual and societal. These patterns are visible not only within the United States but also in societies across the globe where oppression, neglect, and injustice are left unchallenged. There is always cause and effect: the environment shapes the responses of those within it.

Overcoming trauma—racial or otherwise—requires intentional action. Faith, mentorship, community networks, and moral guidance all serve as instruments of resilience. Parents, teachers, and community leaders play critical roles in nurturing discernment, self-respect, and perseverance in young people, providing them with tools to resist cycles of harm. Communities must cultivate support systems that buffer the effects of trauma and empower individuals to transform their lives and surroundings.

The societal consequences of neglecting trauma are profound: mental health struggles, economic instability, and fractured communities all flow from unaddressed harm. Faith can serve as a redemptive force, providing guidance, hope, and strength. For those without faith, human resilience, networks of support, and access to guidance offer alternative paths to agency and purpose. Both avenues, when nurtured, mitigate the destructive impact of trauma and create opportunities for personal and communal restoration.

In a world where racial and systemic trauma are ever-present, the absence of support systems amplifies suffering, often manifesting as violence, rebellion, and social fragmentation. This reality underscores the moral and civic imperative to build networks of care, to provide guidance and mentorship, and to resist injustice wherever it emerges. Faith and human resilience, together or separately, become shields and instruments of transformation—protecting the vulnerable, challenging oppression, and reclaiming dignity in societies too often structured to deny it.

Christian Response

As we close this chapter, we are reminded that God's justice and righteousness are not passive. Scripture calls us **to speak truth, defend the vulnerable, and act justly in every sphere of life.** The challenges explored in this chapter—the legacy of systemic oppression, the cycles of injustice, and the enduring effects of trauma—demand our careful reflection and faithful action.

Psalm 82:3–4 declares, **"Defend the weak and the fatherless; uphold the cause of the poor and the oppressed. Rescue the weak and the needy; deliver them from the hand of the wicked."** This is a divine imperative: to be agents of justice and restoration in our homes, our communities, and in the institutions that shape society.

Romans 12:21 reminds us, **"Do not be overcome by evil, but overcome evil with good."** Even in the face of deep-seated inequities and generational harm, we are called to cultivate goodness, mercy, and righteousness. Acts of faith are not limited to personal devotion—they manifest in service, advocacy, and the pursuit of reconciliation and healing.

Lastly, the lived experiences of racial trauma, injustice, and systemic harm challenge all people of conscience to act. Whether through prayer, mentorship, community service, or faithful witness, *Christians are called to shine light into darkness, to bind wounds, and to embody God's justice in tangible ways.*

> The work is ongoing. The call is clear. Let us move forward with courage, discernment, and unwavering commitment to God's justice, trusting that in every effort to uphold righteousness, we participate in the redemption of both lives and communities.

CHAPTER 6

The Smoke Before the Fire: Rodney King and O.J. Simpson

There are moments in a nation's story when the air thickens long before the flames appear. America in the late 1980s and early 1990s was breathing in that smoke — the warning sign that something deeper was still burning beneath the promise of progress.

The Civil Rights Movement had delivered hard-won victories: the right to vote without humiliation, the end of legalized segregation, and expanded opportunities across education, politics, and economic life. Black Americans and others had marched, bled, and organized their way into a new era where the law finally acknowledged their humanity. There was progress — real and measurable progress.

Yet progress did not extinguish the old fire. It merely brought the buried embers closer.

Beneath the surface of national celebration simmered unresolved trauma — housing discrimination never fully dismantled, economic inequality that widened instead of shrinking, school segregation creeping back under new disguises, and the ongoing targeting of Black communities by policing practices rooted in older systems of control. A generation was raised, then told the fires of racial injustice were dying, while they could still smell the smoke. The smoke was in their neighborhood. The smoke was suffocating every day.

The media, meanwhile, cast its own wind across the nation's perceptions. Crime stories flooded television screens, shaping fear into an evening ritual. Black bodies — whether as suspects or victims — were and are shown as spectacles. The moral panic of drugs, gangs, and "broken neighborhoods" became political fuel. The image of the Black criminal was amplified louder than the voice of the Black citizen.

And then there was the political strategy — *the kindling stacked carefully over time.*

What Richard Nixon called "law and order" and framed as a response to social chaos was carried forward as an unstated but potent racial signal. Ronald Reagan evolved that signal into policy through the War on Drugs — a war that disproportionately arrested and imprisoned Black Americans while claiming to restore safety. George H. W. Bush continued the approach with similar rhetoric. The message remained consistent: crime was the fire endangering America, and the solution was to crack down on the communities most burdened by injustice.

But while politicians to include some Blacks, pointed to the "flames" of crime, they ignored the oxygen feeding the blaze: poverty, discrimination, and decades of systemic neglect.

Each new policy, each televised arrest, each moment of fear-driven messaging acted like lighter fluid poured quietly on dry timber. The public was told the fire was out — but in truth, the coals were expanding. And when coals expand, the smallest spark can become a storm.

The anger and frustration inside marginalized communities weren't spontaneous reactions — they were pressure built over generations. They were laments ignored, stories dismissed, lives undervalued. America kept insisting the fire was from somewhere else — that the heat was coming from the very communities crying out that they were the ones being burned.

Then came the sparks.

The beating of Rodney King in 1991 did not occur in a vacuum — nor did the 1992 Los Angeles uprising erupt out of nothing. Long before that explosion of rage and heartbreak, there had been warning fires: Harlem in 1964, Watts in 1965, Newark and Detroit in 1967, Miami in 1980, and others where police violence, economic abandonment, and racial humiliation ignited communities that could no longer hold in their pain.

Each uprising was a flare signaling the same truth: *The fire never went out — America just refused to see the smoke.*

By the early 1990s, the air was filled with the scent of burning injustice. Political polarization was rising. Racialized fear had once again become a tool of power. And a nation that had congratulated itself on victory over racism was on the verge of learning — violently — that the blaze had only been smoldering, waiting for the wind to shift.

This is the story of that smoke — and of the fire that followed.

— It was not a matter of if a blaze would erupt... but when.

TONY L. SCOTT

The Beating of Rodney King, 1991 – Violence Caught on Camera

The evening of March 3, 1991, in Los Angeles, California, would become a defining moment in the nation's reckoning with race, policing, and the media. Rodney King, a thirty-year-old Black man, was pursued by Los Angeles Police Department officers for speeding. What followed would be recorded on a home video camera, an instrument of unintended justice that captured the brutality of a system steeped in racial bias.

King was pulled from his vehicle and subjected to a prolonged, violent beating by multiple officers. Batons struck him again and again. He was kicked, tasered, and repeatedly assaulted while lying defenseless on the ground. The violence was not only shocking in its severity but in its ordinariness—reflecting a culture within law enforcement where unchecked aggression toward Black citizens was normalized.

The video footage, broadcast nationally, sparked outrage across communities. For many Black Americans, the scene confirmed a lived reality: that the protections promised under law were often absent when the victim was Black. For white Americans, the visual evidence forced a confrontation with something that had long been ignored or rationalized. The immediacy of video brought the violence into living rooms across the country, leaving little room for denial.

This incident highlighted five critical themes that would reverberate far beyond that night. *First,* the visible brutality of law enforcement against Black bodies became undeniable, captured in the stark, unflinching lens of a civilian camera. *Second,* the racialized nature of policing in urban centers was thrust into the national consciousness, showing how implicit biases, departmental cultures, and historical prejudice intersect to produce injustice. *Third,* the power of media to shape public awareness became evident: without that video, the world may have remained oblivious to King's suffering. *Fourth,* the incident underscored the limits of institutional accountability, as the officers involved were not immediately punished, revealing systemic barriers to justice. *Finally,* it revealed the simmering tension in American society, where decades of unresolved racial inequality were ready to erupt under the weight of clear evidence.

Rodney King's beating was not an isolated incident—it was part of a historical continuum of racialized violence in Los Angeles and across the nation. African Americans had long experienced harassment, abuse, and intimidation from law enforcement, and King's ordeal, painfully, became emblematic of a wider truth. The video, for the first time, left little room for dismissal or reinterpretation. It was a moment when the country had to confront the physical manifestation of racial injustice in real time.

King's beating would soon become the catalyst for a far larger eruption of anger and frustration: the 1992 Los Angeles riots. But before we move to that chapter of unrest, it is essential to recognize the gravity of the event itself. This was a moment when violence, race, and media intersected to reveal the fragility of justice and the deep fissures in American society. The beating of Rodney King was not simply about one man—it was a mirror reflecting the nation's ongoing struggle with race, law enforcement, and accountability.

TONY L. SCOTT

The 1992 Los Angeles Riots – Outrage Erupts

The acquittal of the four officers charged in the brutal beating of Rodney King on April 29, 1992, ignited long-simmering tensions across Los Angeles. For Blacks and other communities of color, the verdict was not simply a legal decision; it was a declaration that the system had failed to recognize the humanity of Black citizens. Anger, frustration, and despair, long restrained by patience and hope for justice, erupted into open protest.

What followed was a city in flames. Over six days, Los Angeles experienced some of the most widespread civil unrest in modern American history. Buildings burned, streets became battlegrounds, and highways were blocked by rioters and looters alike. The riots were fueled not only by the acquittal of the officers but by decades of systemic inequities: discriminatory policing, economic marginalization, underfunded schools, and the persistent erosion of trust between communities of color and law enforcement.

The Rodney King riots occurring throughout California and on a lesser scale—demonstrations and minor civil disruptions taking place in other major cities in America, involving various ethnicities revealed a sharp racial divide in public perception and reaction. For many white Americans, the images of looting, burning, and violence became the dominant narrative, often obscuring the systemic injustices that provoked the unrest. For Black Americans, the riots were a visible expression of pent-up anger, grief, and the urgency of a message that had long been ignored. Across the nation, debates flared over law and order versus justice, discipline versus understanding, and the media's portrayal of "rioters" versus "protesters."

The events also exposed the role of politics in interpreting the unrest. Conservative voices seized upon the riots to advance a narrative of disorder and moral decline, echoing the law-and-order rhetoric of prior decades. Meanwhile, some politicians and others sought to temper the conversation, framing the unrest as a call for reform in policing, social services, and economic opportunity. Regardless of perspective, the riots laid bare the gaping chasms in American society, demonstrating that racial grievances could no longer be contained or ignored.

Beyond the immediate destruction, the 1992 riots left a lasting imprint on national consciousness. They were not simply an isolated event but a continuation of a pattern: when the justice system fails to hold those in power accountable, communities are forced to respond in the only ways they view as available to them. The Los Angeles riots became both a warning and a symptom, signaling the urgent need for systemic change while reflecting the persistent failures of society to address the root causes of racial inequality.

Media Portrayal and the Machinery of Division

The media wields extraordinary influence in shaping the consciousness of a society. It is a mirror, a magnifier, and at times a manipulator of public perception. During the O.J. Simpson trial in 1995, that influence was on full display. Simpson, a celebrated Black athlete and cultural icon, stood accused of murdering his ex-wife, Nicole Brown Simpson—a prominent White woman—and her friend, Ronald Goldman.

The spectacle began even before the trial, when millions watched live as television networks broadcast the now-infamous low-speed pursuit of

Simpson's white Ford Bronco, driven by his friend Al Cowlings, as O.J. hid in the backseat, after being named the prime suspect. The nation stood transfixed—some in disbelief, and many others in open enthusiastic support of O.J., which was viewed as the slow chase was captured by news media helicopters, while the vehicle proceeded through Los Angeles highways and streets. The pursuit ended two hours later after Al drove O.J. to his home; there, he was taken into custody.

When the courtroom proceedings began, the racial undertones of the trial became unmistakable. The revelation that Los Angeles police detective Mark Fuhrman had repeatedly used racist slurs and harbored deep prejudice against Black Americans shattered public confidence in the integrity of law enforcement and exposed a deeper wound in the nation's conscience. For months, news coverage, talk shows, and televised commentary dissected every detail, every controversy, and every moment of tension.

While such coverage informed the public, it also shaped narratives that reinforced preexisting racial divisions. Neither did it help that one media outlet had portrayed an altered mugshot of O.J., who was a handsome man; that made him look menacing and sinister. For Black America, the trial echoed long-standing grievances of systemic injustice and biased policing. For White America, media framing often painted the proceedings as a challenge to law and order. The media's power to influence opinion became unmistakably clear, reinforcing racial fault lines and amplifying societal tension.

The necessity of unbiased, truthful reporting cannot be overshadowed by the lure of spectacle or the demand for ratings. Journalistic integrity is not merely a professional standard—it is a moral one, critical to the health of a society. When the media chooses drama over truth, or provocation over principle, it ceases to inform and begins to deform public understanding.

White Alarm and Re-entrenchment: Fear Turns to Reaction

White Alarm and the Social Context

The beating of Rodney King, the O.J. Simpson trial, and the simmering racial tension of the late 20th century left an indelible mark on American society. For many in White America, these events were interpreted not simply as isolated incidents but as evidence of societal change that threatened established power structures. White alarm—the heightened fear of losing social, political, and economic dominance—became the seedbed for organized and ideologically motivated responses. This alarm did not emerge in a vacuum; it was nurtured over decades by cultural conditioning, political rhetoric, and institutional reinforcement.

Militias and Organized Resistance

In reaction to perceived threats, several militias and extremist groups began to gain traction, presenting themselves as defenders of traditional American values while explicitly or implicitly promoting racial hierarchies. Organizations such as the Oath Keepers, the Three Percenters, Proud Boys, there being others, and the (White) Nationalist Movement gained attention during the 1990s and into the 21st century. These groups positioned themselves as protectors of "law and order" and constitutional freedoms, but their underlying ideology often carried white supremacist and Christian nationalist undertones. The rhetoric of these militias, steeped in fear and resistance to social change, was amplified by sympathetic networks and alternative media channels.

Christian Nationalist Influence

Parallel to these militias, public figures and religious leaders who identified with Christian nationalism exerted influence in shaping political and cultural discourse. Individuals such as Pat Robertson, Jerry Falwell Jr., and movements like the Council for National Policy leveraged religious and cultural authority to frame political participation as a so-called moral duty. In doing so, they intertwined faith with nationalist ideology, reinforcing racial hierarchies under the guise of defending "traditional" values. Their messaging contributed to a broader climate of alarm, feeding into white re-entrenchment strategies that resisted racial equality and progressive reform.

Media Amplification

Political operatives and media personalities further magnified white fear and grievance. Figures like Rush Limbaugh, Sean Hannity, Ann Coulter, Tucker Carlson, Sarah Palin, Steve Bannon and Newt Gingrich, while not explicitly associated with militias, provided a platform for messaging that framed racial and social changes as dangerous, unlawful, or morally corrosive. By linking crime, social unrest, and racial progress to personal insecurity and loss of status, this messaging mobilized public sentiment in ways that emboldened extremist organizations, individuals and helped to give rise to Donald Trump and Trumpism.

Legacy and Long-Term Implications

The culmination of these forces—militias, Christian nationalist messaging, amplified political rhetoric, and social-economic segregation—set the stage for the political realignments witnessed in the 21st century. The reactionary movements of the 1980s and 1990s evolved into organized, highly visible political mobilization, exemplified in and giving fertile ground to *The Rise of Trumpism*. These groups and ideologies continue to shape electoral strategies, public policy debates, and social discourse, demonstrating that the fear and grievances of prior decades were not transient but deeply institutionalized and generational.

By naming specific groups and figures, this section highlights how the intergenerational logic of white supremacy continues to influence the present. The alarm and white grievance of the late 20th century have metastasized into a reactive, organized resistance to social progress that remains politically, culturally, and socially consequential.

Lasting Impact on Race Relations

The events of the 1990s — the beating of Rodney King, the Los Angeles rebellion that followed, and the O.J. Simpson trial — did more than shock the nation in their moment. They crystallized a racial divide that persists today. These flashpoints exposed fissures running deep within the American social fabric: a nation divided in its understanding of justice, in its trust of institutions, and in its very interpretation of truth. For many Black Americans, the repeated failures to secure justice revealed that the structures claiming to protect them were instead designed to control and contain them. Trust was not simply weakened; it was shattered.

Those failures did not stay in the past. The past has a way of living in the present, continuing to shape attitudes, expectations, and fears. What unfolded then created a national memory — traumatized and unresolved — that Black communities still carry. Rodney King's battered body and the acquittals of his assailants became symbolic of a justice system unreliable at best and selectively oppressive at worst. Likewise, the televised spectacle of the O.J. Simpson trial did not heal the divide — it highlighted competing realities. A large segment of white America could not fathom a verdict that acquitted Simpson; equally, Black America could not imagine a justice system that would ever treat them fairly. Both responses were born from lived experience. Both revealed a country that, for many, had never agreed on what justice looks like.

Meanwhile, institutions that should have spoken prophetically — including many churches — were silent or neutral when moral clarity was demanded. Silence in the face of injustice is not neutrality but complicity. And that silence left wounds in the national conscience that have yet to heal.

History, when remembered honestly, functions as testimony — not nostalgia. It warns us. It invites accountability. It forces us to confront uncomfortable truths so that they do not become recurring nightmares. *But when history is denied or softened, the seeds of past injustices germinate in present soil.* The racial fear, resentment, and backlash that simmered throughout the 1990s did not disappear — they matured into a political identity.

It is here that the connection to our current moment becomes unavoidable. Under the presidency of Donald Trump, those unresolved racial tensions have been reactivated and weaponized. When Trump proclaims that he will "Make America Great Again," the slogan is heard differently across racial lines, and rightly so. For many of his supporters, it is a nostalgia-soaked promise to return to a time when American identity was unchallenged by multiculturalism and civil rights gains — before the election of Barack Obama signaled the possibility of a somewhat white America. For Black Americans and other marginalized communities, the message is clear: greatness is defined by a return to white racial hierarchies and social dominance that once went unquestioned.

Thus, the present political climate is not a rupture with history — it is the continuation of it. Trumpism did not invent racial fear and grievance; it simply provided a new platform, a new permission structure, and a national microphone. The storyline that emerged in the 1990s — fear of Black resistance, anxiety over shifting demographics, suspicion of the justice system from both sides, and a media environment capable of shaping reality — has returned with intensified force.

The logic of the past is alive in the present. And unless truth is faced, acknowledged, and answered, it will continue to negatively shape the future as well.

From Reaction to Revelation

History leaves footprints on the soul of a nation.

The events of the 1990s — Rodney King, the uprising in Los Angeles, the trial of O.J. Simpson, and the political responses that followed — were not isolated eruptions of chaos, but revelations of a deeper spiritual crisis. What some saw as disorder was, in truth, the groaning of a people long denied justice. Scripture teaches that **"righteousness exalts a nation,"** but when unrighteousness is protected and defended, the land trembles under its weight. For America, the fire and smoke of that decade were warnings — early signs that what we refused to confront would only grow stronger, louder, and more destructive. And now, under the current presidency of Donald Trump, the past has shown that it never truly passed – America is currently at a major crossroad and crisis; a powder keg ready to explode! The sins we fail to reckon with become the sins that rule us. Therefore, as believers, we must look not only at what happened, but what God is calling His people to do in response — with courage, truth, and a faith that refuses to be silent.

Christian Response

If the 1990s taught us anything, it is that injustice thrives where the Church goes quiet. Far too many pulpits traded prophetic truth for political comfort; far too many Christians chose proximity to power over solidarity with the oppressed. Yet Christ has never permitted His followers to remain neutral in the face of suffering. Jesus stepped into spaces where pain was ignored. He touched the untouchable, defended the abused, confronted corrupt authority, and proclaimed liberty to the captives.

The Church today must rediscover that calling.

We must affirm that Black lives matter to God — not as a slogan, but as a theological truth rooted in the Imago Dei—or the very imagers of God. We must reject systems that criminalize Black bodies while excusing white violence. We must denounce the manipulation of fear — especially when fear is used to sanctify racism. We must walk in boldness, remembering the cross not only as a symbol of salvation, but also as God's public protest against injustice.

Finally, we must embrace the ministry of remembrance. The past is not our enemy — forgetting it is; this truth, under Donald Trump, now sits before us in the White House. When we remember rightly, we see clearly the work that remains. When we repent sincerely, we live as agents of reconciliation. And when we love courageously, we refuse to bow before the idols of race, nationalism, or political power.

> ***For where the Spirit of the Lord is, there is freedom*** — not only for the soul, but for the streets, the systems, and the society God calls us to transform.

CHAPTER 7

God, Family, Country: The Rise of Christian Nationalism and the Politics of Fear

Christian Nationalism Comes Out of the Shadows

God, Family, Country as a Religious-Political Identity. By the late 1990s and early 2000s, a distinct fusion of faith and nationalism began stepping into the public square with renewed boldness. "God, Family, and Country" for many conservative whites became more than a value statement — it was a litmus test for belonging, a badge of who was considered a true American. Churches, especially within white evangelical spaces, preached patriotism not as civic pride but as divine identity. Christianity was and continues to be wrongly increasingly equated with Americanism, as if God's covenant rested specifically on the soil of the United States.

To be Christian was to be loyal to the flag. To challenge America's past — especially its racial sins — was to be viewed as attacking God's chosen nation. The blending of theology and nationalism birthed a movement where faith justified power, and power defended faith, each strengthening the other.

The Myth of a Christian Founding and the Golden Past

Christian nationalism presented a romanticized retelling of American origins. It proclaimed that the United States was founded as a Christian nation, blessed uniquely by God, and destined to lead the world morally. Missing from this myth, of course, was the truth: America's earliest wealth was extracted through stolen land, stolen labor, and stolen lives.

Yet in sermons and political speeches, slavery, Native genocide, and Jim Crow were dismissed as distant "mistakes" rather than as foundational systems shaping modern America. This selective memory served a purpose — if the past was pure, then present racial hierarchies must be righteous. And if God ordained America's rise, then whoever sought to reform it was cast as an enemy of God's order.

Mainstreaming of White Grievance Through Churches

As demographics shifted and immigration increased, many white Christians interpreted these changes spiritually — and fearfully. Sermons described a nation "under attack," not from foreign armies but from cultural equality. Declining white population share became framed as declining righteousness.

Economic frustrations — job loss, neighborhood change, political shifts — were spiritualized. Pastors and religious broadcasters warned congregations: "Your faith is being pushed out. You are being replaced." Churches became political mobilization centers, turning personal insecurity into communal grievance. The ballot box was preached as a battleground for the soul of the nation.

Early Alliances with Conservative Power Brokers

Strategists recognized the immense political force of a fearful, united religious bloc. Republican leaders sharpened messaging that signaled protection of Christianity, even when policies contradicted Christ's teachings. "Law and order," border protection, and resistance to multicultural education became religious causes rather than partisan ones.

Think tanks, legal organizations, and media networks produced materials reinforcing a singular message:

Political power must be seized to preserve Christian America. Thus, a decades-long alliance was cemented — one not rooted in Scripture, but in mutual ambition.

Prophets of a New Dominion – The New Apostolic Reformation

Alongside traditional evangelicalism, a newer movement emerged with explosive influence: the New Apostolic Reformation (NAR). Its leaders claimed modern-day apostolic authority — so-called prophets who heard directly from God regarding national destiny.

They preached that Christians were called to take dominion over the "Seven Mountains" of cultural power:

1. Government

2. Education
3. Media
4. Business
5. Arts and Entertainment
6. Religion
7. Family

This was not evangelism — it was conquest. The United States was framed as territory to reclaim for God. Opponents were cast not simply as political adversaries but as spiritual enemies. Winning elections became holy warfare.

The NAR movement provided the spiritual language that would later elevate political figures — including Donald Trump — as divinely chosen instruments, regardless of character or morality. Their rise marked a shift from persuasion to domination, from faith as witness to faith as weapon.

Conservative Media as Radicalization Engine – Fox News, Rush Limbaugh, and the Outrage Machine

By the 1990s, the American media landscape had moved beyond nightly network news. Cable television, syndicated talk radio, and then the early internet created an ecosystem in which outrage could be packaged, repeated, and monetized. Out of that ecosystem emerged a new kind of political communication: not measured argument so much as performance—a continuous loop of grievance, alarm, and moral certainty.

Three powerful features defined this engine:

1. **Framing and Repetition.** Outlets and personalities framed news stories through a narrow set of lenses—immigration as invasion, urban unrest as moral collapse, and multiculturalism as cultural erasure. Repetition made the frame familiar; familiarity made it seem common sense. When viewers heard the same warnings day after day, fear graduated into conviction.

2. **Personalized Outrage and Moral Panic.** Hosts like Rush Limbaugh pioneered an intimate, combative radio style that treated listeners as kin—victims of liberal elites, secular media, and a changing America. Cable opinion television shows amplified that tone visually, creating heroes and villains and urging immediate action. Moral panic about crime, family breakdown, and declining values became staple programming.

3. **Mobilization Infrastructure.** Beyond rhetoric, the media built institutions—call-in shows, mailing lists, telemarketing drives, donor networks, and audience analytics—that converted listeners into activists and voters. Evangelical leaders were courted and given platforms; the pulpit and the airwaves became mutually reinforcing. The result was a politically energized, media-literate voting bloc that could be activated quickly for campaigns and causes framed as existential.

Alongside these techniques was a steady stream of selective storytelling: dramatic episodes of crime or scandal were presented as representative trends; social policy failures were offered as proof that liberal governance had failed. The storytelling rarely acknowledged structural causes—

poverty, segregation, chronic underinvestment—and instead focused blame on cultural decline or deliberate malice. That narrative made punitive responses sound not only reasonable but righteous.

The media's role was not merely to inform. It constructed enemies, sanctified grievances, and offered simple remedies: tougher policing, stricter immigration rules, and a cultural reaffirmation of "traditional" values. Those prescriptions found eager listeners in communities anxious about change. Over time, the outrage machine normalized a politics in which every cultural shift could be read as a threat—and every threat required a firm, often punitive, response.

The Revival of White-Power Movements – Militias, Identity, and the Digital Turn

Where the conservative media provided grievance and organization, an overlapping set of movements provided arms, doctrine, and direct action. The 1990s saw a notable resurgence of anti-government and white-power activity, especially after the Oklahoma City bombing in 1995—a violent act that both alarmed the nation and galvanized sympathetic underground networks.

Important dynamics in this revival:

- *From Posse to Patriots*: The modern militia movement drew on an older tradition—Posse Comitatus and regional anti-government activism—but it reorganized into decentralized local cells, self-defense fantasies, and paramilitary training. "Patriot" language reframed militias as defenders of liberty, not racists; the rhetoric of defense made recruitment easier in communities where distrust of government had historical roots.

- *Christian Identity and the Sanctification of Race*: In many strands, white-power ideology fused with religious language. Some groups invoked Christian Identity or similar theological strains to claim divine sanction for racial hierarchy. Others used more mainstream evangelical codes ("preserving family," "protecting heritage") to cloak racial aims. The effect was to make white supremacy appear less as explicit hate and more as urgent moral preservation.

- *Post-Oklahoma Growth*: The aftermath of the Oklahoma City bombing was paradoxical. The violent act exposed the danger of extremism, but it also drew attention to the very networks that produced it. Militia activity—training, recruitment, and local organizing—grew in pockets across rural and exurban America. Local preparedness fairs, paramilitary forums, and survivalist gatherings became recruitment grounds.

- *The Internet and Normalization*: Crucially, the late 1990s and early 2000s saw the internet move from niche bulletin boards into mainstream usage. Message boards, chat rooms, and later social media spaces enabled rapid dissemination of conspiracy theories and allowed isolated actors to find communities. Over time, themes once confined to fringe pamphlets—replacement fears, anti-government conspiracies, race-based grievances—migrated into broader networks, achieving a chilling normalization.

- *Cross-Pollination with Mainstream Politics*: As media outlets legitimized certain grievances and the online world amplified them, there was steady cross-pollination. Members of militias and extremist chat spaces found sympathetic voices in talk radio and cable punditry. Political operatives learned to harness that energy—sometimes subtly, sometimes overtly—turning discontent into votes and, in some tragic cases, into action.

How the Two Engines Fed Each Other

These forces—media outrage and militant revival—did not operate in isolation. They fed one another in a self-reinforcing cycle:

- Media amplified a narrative of decline and threat, producing audiences primed to accept radical solutions.

- Militias and conspiracy networks offered action, identity, and a sense of control to those frightened by the stories.

- Digital platforms shrank the distance between talk and action, allowing recruitment, coordination, and escalation.

- Political actors, recognizing an energized base, began to use the rhetoric and sometimes the strategies of these networks for electoral advantage.

The net effect was striking: grievance migrated from private fear to public politics, and from marginal subcultures into the mainstream. What had once been fringe became, in stages, a powerful current in American life—one that would contribute directly to the political realignments and violent flashpoints of the next decades.

The Moral and Practical Stakes

This convergence—outrage media and organized, often armed, grievance—did more than produce bad ideas. It shaped institutions: pressuring law enforcement priorities, influencing local politics, and altering civic norms about protest and dissent. It also created a moral crisis for religious communities: when the pulpit and the airwaves insist that political power is sacred, the Church's prophetic voice is weakened and its witness compromised.

The path forward demands clear diagnosis: acknowledge how stories shape fear, how fear breeds identity politics, and how identity politics can become a vehicle for coercion and violence. In the following sections, we will examine how these developments moved from rhetoric to policy, and from localized networks to national movements—setting the stage for the political transformations that would follow in the Obama era and beyond.

The Theology of Manifest Destiny, Reborn

The belief that America was chosen—set apart by God for a people destined to rule—never vanished after the 19th century. It simply changed clothes. The same theological justification that once propelled European settlers across Turtle Island (North America), claiming land already inhabited by Indigenous nations, began to show up anew in 20th and 21st-century political rhetoric.

The divine permission granted to "explore, conquer, and possess" did not remain trapped in old textbooks; it reemerged as a conviction that God Himself authored white dominance over the American landscape. No matter how history exposes the brutality of colonization—the massacres, the forced removals, the cultural erasures—the narrative is continually reframed as a sacred pilgrimage, a righteous journey ordained from heaven. Under this perverted worldview, America belongs to white Christians not merely by law or power, but by divine right.

And with divine right comes divine hierarchy. The religious nationalism of the era cast white male identity as the head of the national household and others as God-assigned subordinates. The language becomes subtle: "heritage," "values," "law and order," "saving America." These are virtue-draped phrases that mask an older, darker creed—one that insists God established racial tiers and placed the white Christian male at its apex. History is curated to support this vision. Scripture is selectively cited to present America as a new Israel, and whiteness as the chosen lineage. Evangelical leaders, Christian radio commentators, and political operatives find common theological ground in this claim: To resist white rule in America is to rebel against God.

The story is carefully sanitized. The blood of Indigenous peoples and the sweat of enslaved Africans are removed from the narrative stage. Schoolbooks speak of bravery, pioneering spirit, and American exceptionalism—while genocide and chattel slavery are filed under "controversial topics" or erased entirely. Patriotism becomes a theological shield—a sanctified smoke screen—that blinds a nation to the atrocities upon which its freedom was built. In this reborn Manifest Destiny, America is pure because the narrative says so, God-favored because the majority declares it, innocent because its history is edited. And those who question this mythology are recast as enemies—anti-American, anti-Christian, divisive. The story must remain heroic if the power it protects is to remain unquestioned.

White Christian nationalism does not thrive on truth; it thrives on memory—carefully crafted, fervently defended memory. As long as the nation's origin story is wrapped in divine perfection, the movement can wrongly claim that its struggle to maintain social dominance is not prejudice but prayer, not supremacy but stewardship. This is the mythic foundation upon which a new wave of political and religious activism prepares to stand... and strike.

By the dawn of the 21st century, the convergence of power, fear, theology, and media had reshaped American identity. The believed or so-called "righteous anger" of white Christians did not emerge in a vacuum—it was cultivated, reinforced, and sanctified. This was not simply a resurgence of a political faction, but the unveiling of a belief system that saw America's changing face as a sign of divine crisis. And when crisis meets conviction, movements ignite. What was once whispered in private meetings and broadcast on fringe radio now marched boldly into the public square. White Christian nationalism stepped forward—not ashamed, not uncertain, but determined to reclaim what it believed God had given exclusively to them.

Christian Response

If the Church forgets the truth about its past, it will lose its witness in the present. The gospel of Jesus Christ has never been about racial hierarchy or national dominion. The Kingdom of God is not America—and whiteness is not a covenant. To follow Christ faithfully, believers must confront the idols that have masqueraded as faith: power, dominance, and patriotic mythology. The call of Christ is not to preserve privilege but to proclaim a kingdom where every tribe, every tongue, every nation stands equal at the foot of the cross. The Church must repent of the lies it has blessed, expose the false gods draped in flags, and reclaim the gospel—not for the sake of a nation, but for the sake of the world God loves.

CHAPTER 8

The Great Replacement: Panic, Suppression, Revision, and the Struggle for Power

Demographic Anxiety Becomes Crisis Rhetoric

By the turn of the 21st century, something more than changing statistics was circulating through political texts, church basements, talk radio, and conservative mailing lists: an existential narrative about the nation's future. Census reports and demographic projections—presented in plain tables and footnotes—were read in a different key by commentators and strategists who did not treat numbers as neutral facts but as moral warnings. The dry language of "majority-minority" shifts became, for many, an alarm bell: the country they recognized was not just changing; it was being stolen from them.

This anxiety had several features worth noting because they shaped how policy and politics unfolded afterwards:

- *Numbers as Narrative.* Census projections that showed growth among Latino, Black, Asian, and multiracial populations were translated from statistical charts into stories about replacement. Headlines and soundbites displaced methodological nuance. A graph of birthrates or immigration flows was no longer data for planners; it became proof of a cultural and political threat.

- *Emotional Framing of Demography.* Demographic change is inherently neutral. What turned it into crisis rhetoric was the emotional frame applied to it. Instead of focusing on integration, opportunity, or pluralism, commentators emphasized decline—decline of culture, of moral standards, of political control. This framing made anxiety contagious: uncertainty about jobs or schools found a convenient target in shifting population numbers.

- *Political Entrepreneurs and the Marketplace of Fear.* There were entrepreneurs of fear—media personalities, consultants, think tanks—who turned demographic anxiety into a marketable product. Books, radio segments, and cable segments sold certainty: a simple explanation for complex social change and a prescribed remedy—vote differently, legislate differently, protect borders, preserve culture. Fear became a commodity that could be monetized and mobilized.

- *The Role of Local Experience.* For many Americans, especially in the postindustrial and rural counties hollowed out by deindustrialization, demographic change arrived wrapped in real loss—loss of steady employment, tax base, and a sense of control. Demographic anxieties, therefore, nested easily inside economic distress; the change in population served as a visible symbol for a deeper sense of dispossession.

- *Institutional Echo Chambers.* Once anxiety had been amplified by media and political entrepreneurs, institutions amplified it further. Churches that had already married cultural conservatism to theology repeated warnings from the pulpit. School boards, civic groups, and grassroots organizations absorbed and transmitted the message. The result was a broad ecosystem of suspicion that did not rely solely on elite channels—fear was now diffuse and locally rooted.

The rhetorical consequence was clear: what had once been projection exercises for planners and policymakers became existential warnings for entire populations. The danger of this shift is not merely rhetorical. When demographic change is framed as catastrophe, the political remedies are rarely constructive integration or democratic inclusion. Instead, they are preservationist: restriction, exclusion, and the re-engineering of political power to slow or reverse the demographic trend. Once numbers become moral threats, policy becomes a war of containment.

"We Are Losing Our Country" Becomes a Conservative Slogan

From the diffuse anxiety about demography emerged a simple, repeatable refrain—powerful precisely because of its simplicity: We are losing our country. The phrase condensed a wealth of fears—economic, cultural, racial, and civic—into a rallying cry. It was not merely descriptive; it was a call to arms.

How did a sentence become a movement?

Several mechanisms explain the transformation:

- *Slogans as Political Technology.* Political movements rely on shorthand. Long arguments lose traction; short, emotive phrases travel. "We are losing our country" performed politically: it was repeatable, mobilizing, and morally urgent. The slogan could be invoked in a speech, on a bumper sticker, in a sermon, or at a town-hall meeting, carrying with it the full freight of threat and remedy.

- *Moral Language Meets Political Instrumentalism.* The phrase worked because it used moral language to justify political ends. Losing the country implied not just electoral loss but spiritual failure—a civilization slipping from the hands of its "rightful stewards." That moral register allowed leaders to propose political remedies as moral imperatives rather than partisan options.

- *Across-the-Board Applications.* The slogan was flexible. It could be applied to immigration policy, cultural debates, school curricula, or judicial appointments. Its elasticity made it a universal foil for any change a conservative base disliked: the loss of manufacturing jobs could be blamed on globalization or demographic shifts; a new school curriculum could be framed as an assault on heritage. The slogan created a single antagonistic logic that unified otherwise disparate grievances.

- *Mobilizing a Voting Bloc.* Above all, the phrase helped convert anxiety into votes. It turned private resentment into public action: attend rallies, sign petitions, show up at school board meetings, and above all, go to the polls. Political operatives recognized how effective the slogan could be in directory-building and turnout—especially among suburban and rural voters who felt newly vulnerable.

- *Celebrity Endorsements and Political Amplification.* When influential voices repeated the slogan—radio hosts, cable personalities, pastors, and eventually politicians—it gained legitimacy. Political actors learned that echoing the phrase signaled alignment with a large, motivated constituency. Over time, the slogan moved from the margins of talk radio into mainstream Republican messaging.

- *Legitimizing Policy Tools of Exclusion.* The rhetorical frame paved the way for policy. If the country was at stake, then extraordinary measures were justified: tightened immigration controls, aggressive deportation policies, voter ID laws framed as anti-fraud (but deployed where they suppressed likely opposition), and aggressive redistricting to lock in power. The slogan's moral urgency helped normalize policies that, in calmer moments, would be subjected to greater democratic scrutiny.

This slogan did not invent the politics that followed; it catalyzed them. It provided language that allowed an array of tactics—legal, political, cultural—to be seen as defensive rather than offensive. Framed as defense, even hardline measures of exclusion could be spoken of as temporary necessities to save a nation, even so, strategies to cement dominance.

Having laid out how demographic data and white anxiety were weaponized into a political refrain, we are now prepared to see the next step: a conspiratorial theory that gave the anxiety a clear villain and therefore a direct enemy to oppose. The story moves from fear of change to accusation of deliberate design—the shape that would be taken by the Great Replacement narrative in the United States.

Great Replacement Theory in U.S. Form

If demographic anxiety provided the emotional spark, the Great Replacement Theory provided the storyline—a narrative claiming that demographic change was not natural or organic but orchestrated. Imported from far-right European discourse, the U.S. version adapted the idea into an especially racial framework:

Immigration was not a movement — it was invasion.
Diversity was not growth — it was erasure.
Policy was not debate — it was conspiracy.

Immigration as Intentional Racial Invasion

In political ads, cable news segments, and speeches, immigration — particularly from Mexico, Central America, Africa, and the Caribbean — was described as a threat to "our way of life." The border became the symbolic front line of protecting not merely safety, but whiteness. Immigrants were framed as agents of demographic displacement, sent by political actors determined to undermine white political dominance. The language escalated: from "swarms" to "hordes," from "illegals" to "invaders" and "criminals." This rhetoric turned human beings into weapons.

Cultural and Religious Paranoia

As the nation grew more pluralistic, fear-based appeals cast Christianity itself as endangered. Bilingual education, changes in holiday language, or growth in non-Christian worship were framed as signs of cultural overwhelm.

The narrative insisted:

If immigrants reshape culture, then the dominant faith will fall. This fusion of cultural and religious anxiety became the theological fuel powering political radicalism.

Islamophobia Post-9/11

After the attacks of September 11, 2001, Islamophobia intensified exponentially. Muslims — and anyone who appeared Middle Eastern, South Asian, or North African — were cast as existential dangers. Policies such as the Patriot Act, "no-fly lists," and surveillance of mosques were rationalized as necessary protections. The fear metastasized into a broader narrative: not just that terrorists were coming, but that Muslims were part of a takeover — a religious component within the Great Replacement myth. Anti-Muslim prejudice became a sanctioned form of bigotry within mainstream politics.

Expansion of Vigilante Border Militias

The idea of "invasion" naturally led to "defense." Civilians — many armed, often self-appointed, and largely white — formed militias claiming to "secure the border where the government failed." Groups like the Minuteman Project patrolled the Southwest desert armed with rifles and night-vision equipment. Their activities normalized a dangerous belief: that ordinary citizens had both the authority and moral obligation to enforce racial boundaries. Law and order became a grassroots crusade — untethered from legal accountability.

These strands converged into a single conspiratorial script: white Americans were being replaced by design, and only vigilant resistance could stop it. A concept once confined to extremist pamphlets had now entered political campaigns and prime-time broadcasts. It would not remain fringe — it was becoming a governing worldview.

Voter Suppression as Political Strategy

If demographic shifts threatened white political control through legitimate participation, then restricting participation became a logical political response. Instead of expanding democracy to accommodate demographic change, conservative strategists devised schemes to shape the electorate rather than win it.

Restrictive ID Laws and Gerrymandering

Under the guise of preventing voter fraud — a statistically negligible phenomenon — states introduced strict identification requirements known to disproportionately burden Black, Latino, young, and low-income voters. Gerrymandered districts fractured or diluted minority communities, allowing shrinking white populations to retain power disproportionate to their numbers. Mathematical precision was used to engineer political inequality.

Polling Place Closures in Black Communities

By reducing the number of polling sites in densely populated and minority neighborhoods, states manufactured the conditions for long lines, excessive wait times, and discouraged turnout. Meanwhile, white suburban precincts retained ample access. The message was implicit but clear: some votes are meant to be easier than others.

Voter Roll Purges

Aggressive voter roll purging — often targeting those with similar names, inactive voting history, or mismatched databases — purged thousands of eligible voters, especially in majority-Black counties. Errors were not merely accidental; the system was designed to err in a particular direction.

Reduced Early Voting and Absentee Options

Early voting — a crucial tool for workers, caregivers, and those with limited transportation — was restricted. Sunday voting, especially significant for "Souls to the Polls" initiatives driven by Black churches, was curtailed in several states. By targeting the methods disproportionately used by minority voters, power was protected without ever altering the Constitution.

Additional Tactics of Exclusion

- Disinformation campaigns aimed at minority populations
- Legal threats to immigrant communities, naturalized citizens, and formerly incarcerated persons

- The elevation of false claims of voter fraud to justify future suppression

Each tactic alone could be defended as "administrative." Together, they form a systemic strategy: to slow or prevent the political empowerment that demographic reality would otherwise produce.

With demographic shifts framed as invasion and political participation treated as a threat, the next move became inevitable: control the story of the country itself. To maintain power, history would need to be rewritten — or erased.

Whitewashing the Past to Control the Present

History is not merely a record of what happened — it is the story a nation decides to tell about itself. When that story threatens the foundations of power, those in control often revise, sanitize, or erase the parts that expose injustice. In the struggle to preserve white dominance amid changing demographics, control of historical narrative became a battleground.

Resistance to Teaching Slavery, Jim Crow, and Systemic Racism

Across school boards, state legislatures, and conservative media, a new apologetics emerged: protecting students from the so-called "divisiveness" of truth. Proposals to teach the full brutality of slavery, the violence of Reconstruction's overthrow, and the intentionality of Jim Crow laws were recast as attacks on patriotism. Educators faced censorship for naming racism, while books documenting oppression were banned under the language of "parental rights."

The aim was not ignorance — it was amnesia crafted to preserve racial innocence.

Undermining Black Achievement in History — The Oldest Erasure

Efforts to erase Black excellence did not begin in the United States. This project is rooted in colonization itself. European imperial powers crafted a narrative that Africa was a continent without history, without innovation, without civilization — a lie necessary to justify conquest.

- Advanced pre-colonial kingdoms such as Mali, Songhai, Benin, Great Zimbabwe, Kongo, and Axum demonstrated sophisticated economies, social governance, engineering, architecture, and global scholarship.

- Universities such as Timbuktu's Sankoré drew students from across the Islamic world centuries before European Enlightenment.

- Medical, astronomical, agricultural, and artistic advancements flourished long before Europe claimed itself as civilization's birthplace.

To colonize land, European empires first colonized imagination. They imposed a mythology of African primitiveness so that the theft of land, resources, and human beings could appear as rescue, not robbery. This colonial erasure followed the stolen millions into the Americas.

Enslaved Africans were portrayed as labor, not knowledgeable; as property, not people; as a workforce with no history worth remembering.

Even after emancipation, Black progress — scientific inventions, political leadership, military valor, cultural artistry, economic growth — was routinely hidden, dismissed, or credited to white intermediaries.

If history acknowledged Black brilliance and Black survival, then white supremacy — the ideological core of the American project — would crumble.

"Heritage Not Hate" – Patriotism as Cover for Oppression

The Confederate cause, once a rebellion against the United States, was reframed into a nostalgic story of regional pride. Monuments to traitorous leaders were erected not after the Civil War, but during Jim Crow and the Civil Rights Movement — political statements that white dominance would stand unmoved. The Confederate flag was elevated as sacred cloth, patriotism weaponized against accountability.

"Heritage not hate" became the slogan used to protect symbols created explicitly to enforce racial terror. It was not history being preserved — but hierarchy.

To maintain power in an era of demographic shift, shaping the past was only part of the plan. The next step was shaping the present through media weaponization and the merging of religious identity with white nationalism.

Conservative Media Finishes Mainstreaming Extremism

Reinforcing its inception and continuing divisive and dangerous impact. In the media ecosystem of the 2000s and 2010s, so it was fear became the product and outrage the delivery mechanism. Terms like "illegals," "criminals," "thugs," and "terrorists" were repeated on talk radio and cable news until they lost the shock of meaning—and instead became identifiers for entire populations. One of the most explicit examples of this shift came in January 2018 when President Donald Trump reportedly asked, "Why are we having all these people from shithole countries come here?"—referring to Haiti and nations in Africa. The remark sent shock waves worldwide, but within the media loops that had long normalized racist tropes, it functioned as reinforcement of a narrative: some people come from places unworthy of white America.

This moment illustrates several features of how fear-based media narratives were weaponized:

- *Visibility of Hate through Policy Discourse*: The remark wasn't shouted in a bar—it came from the Oval Office in a conversation about immigration reform. That context meant the language was not dismissed as individual bigotry, but recast as policy-relevant truth.

- *Elevating Illicit Populations into National Threats*: By pointing at entire nations and populations as undesirable, the media repeated the idea that others are threats to American well-being. This logic blurred the line between criminal justice and immigrant identity;

being brown or foreign became almost synonymous with being dangerous.

- *Mobilization Strategy*: It wasn't enough to say society was changing—it had to be framed as under attack. Media anchors and pundits echoed the sentiment, directing white audiences' anxieties outward. Once the message of threat took hold, the mobilization of votes, of activism, of militia mentality became easier.

- *Conspiracies Made Palatable*: What once was fringe—immigration as a takeover, Muslims as infiltrators, demographic change as orchestrated—moved into the mainstream via repeating loops on news shows, talk radio, and later social media. The conspiratorial nature was hidden by repetition and authority. The listener's question became: "If it's repeated so much, maybe it's true."

- *White Identity as Sacred Identity*: In this ecosystem, white Christian identity was framed not just as the cultural majority but as holy inheritance. Media messages told viewers they were not simply Americans—they were defenders of America's Christian soul. Churches echoed this, pastors preached about foundations being undermined, and networks amplified the message of civilizational decline tied to racial change.

- *Defenders of American Christianity*: When Christianity fused with whiteness in these narratives, militant language followed. The defender motif framed Christianity as under siege by secularism, multiculturalism, and non-white populations. Protecting faith became indistinguishable from protecting race. Talk radio described the United States as a "Christian nation" that would not survive without white leadership. Militias and parishioners alike believed they were standing guard.

The tactics and matters at hand were calculated. By the time the first decade of the 2000s ended, mainstream conservative media had accomplished a transformation: what was once fringe extremist talk had moved into prime-time respectability. The shift was not just rhetorical—it was structural. Audiences had grown comfortable with articulate rage. Political figures and media hosts no longer had to signal subtly; the sentiment of preservation of whiteness was openly voiced. The stage was set for the next wave of action—not only political campaigns and laws, but movement politics, activism, and violence.

Militia + Christian Nationalism Convergence

As the post-9/11 era evolved into the Obama years, a dangerous spiritual-political fusion took shape: armed militias began to wrap themselves in Christian purpose, and Christian nationalism found muscle in armed militias. The disciples of fear merged with the disciples of dominion — and both arrogantly and falsely claimed Jesus as their Commander-in-Chief.

White Identity Becomes "Sacred Identity"

This convergence is fueled by a mythic belief: that white Americans — particularly white Christians — are chosen stewards of a divine national order.

In this worldview:

- White existence equals Christian existence.
- American culture equals biblical culture.
- Any shift in demographics becomes an attack on God Himself.

Scripture is misused as a barricade — not a bridge.
Citizenship becomes covenant.
Whiteness becomes worship.

The nation is seen as the last standing bastion of "biblical civilization," and those who challenge white power are branded as enemies of God and state.

Defenders of "American Christianity"

As political rhetoric grows apocalyptic — "Take our country back!" "They are replacing us!" — militias position themselves as holy protectors of what they deem as a collapsing Christian nation. They train with rifles while quoting Paul. They march in tactical gear while carrying crosses. They declare:

"We are defending Christianity!"

But what they defend is not the gospel — it is a system of power.
They are not defenders of justice — they are militarized culture warriors.
Their theology is not from Jesus — it is from Jericho, minus the command to lay down the sword.

Even some Black and Brown Christians are pulled into this distortion — seduced by promises of belonging, status, or shared social conservatism — despite being aligned with a movement built to exclude them.

What emerges is a shadow church:

- Patriotism preached as salvation
- Race preserved as righteousness
- Guns held with more conviction than grace
- A Lamb replaced by a flag-draped lion of vengeance

A Christianity that must be defended with violence has already abandoned the Christ who refused it.

Christian Response

The Church must see clearly what is at stake:
The cross is being replaced by a sword.
Faith is being remade into nationalism.

Skin and culture are being enthroned where Christ alone should reign.

Therefore, the Church must stand firm in the following truths:

Our Identity Is in Christ — Not in Whiteness, Borders, or Flags

Paul declared:

"Here there is neither Jew nor Greek… but Christ is all, and in all."
(Colossians 3:11)

The minute Christianity demands ethnic or national loyalty, it ceases to be Christian.

Power Is Not Proof of God's Favor

Jesus rebuked Peter for taking up the sword:

"Put your sword back in its place."
(Matthew 26:52)

Political dominance is not discipleship.

Victory at the polls is not vindication of righteousness.

Fear Cannot Be Our Evangelist

Perfect love casts out fear — but fear has become a gospel in many pulpits.

The Church must expose this false doctrine:

Fear of immigrants is not holiness.
Fear of history is not righteousness.
Fear of losing power is not faith — it is idolatry.

The Kingdom Is Not America

Jesus made it plain:

"My Kingdom is not of this world."
(John 18:36)

Any church seeking to "protect Christianity" by force has declared that the Kingdom of God needs their weapons to survive — a theological impossibility and a spiritual insult.

The Call Forward

Christians must reject the merging of the cross and the Constitution.
We must dismantle every narrative that baptizes race or nationalism.
We must reclaim the gospel from political hijacking.

To be the Church is not to defend power — it is to witness to truth, to practice justice,

and to love all nations or peoples.

The only Christian nation is the one John saw in Revelation:

"A great multitude… from every nation, tribe, and people, and language…"
(Revelation 7:9)

This is the Kingdom we represent.
This is the future we live for.
This is the witness we must give — boldly, sacrificially, and without compromise.

CHAPTER 9

The Obama Effect
and
The Counter-Revolution Against Hope

November 4, 2008. The Nation Held Its Breath

In Chicago's Grant Park, faces glistened with tears — elders who survived Jim Crow clutching hands with grandchildren who had only known post-Civil Rights America. Across Black churches nationwide, watch parties felt like Sunday services: choirs humming, deacons praying, mothers whispering "Thank You, Lord." This was not just an election result — it was a public sigh of relief from many who had believed their citizenship required proof, approval, if belonging at all.

Barack Hussein Obama — a Black man with an African father and white mother, had a name that sounded nothing like the presidents in American history books — became the 44th President of the United States.

But while millions rejoiced, others retreated into quiet — and not-so-quiet — panic and grievance. On conservative media platforms, the celebration was framed as a threat. A shift. A loss. A moment when America — their America — slipped from their grasp. The moment that felt like progress for many felt like dispossession for others. And that fear would be given shape, voice, and direction.

On that cold January morning in 2009, millions pressed together along the National Mall — Black families and others wrapped in blankets, veterans in wheelchairs draped in flags, young students holding homemade cardboard signs with a single word painted in blue: Hope. From the steps of the Capitol, surrounded by the monuments built with slave labor and dedicated to liberty, a Black man prepared to place his hand on a Bible once held by Abraham Lincoln and speak the oath of a nation that had never fully accepted his humanity.

Grandmothers who had survived Jim Crow wept openly. Children climbed onto their fathers' shoulders to see a living miracle. The world watched as the United States — the nation that had auctioned African bodies, enforced segregation, and resisted equality at every turn — swore in Barack Hussein Obama as its 44th president. For many, it felt like history turning a corner it had too long resisted.

But history does not move in straight lines.

In diners in the rural South and in living rooms of the Rust Belt, televisions were tuned in to the same speech — and not everyone watching saw hope. Some saw a threat: a Black man elevated to the highest place in the land, they believed, belonged to them. A quiet unrest stirred. Conversations behind closed doors hardened into certainty. The unspoken fears of white decline — demographic change, cultural shift — were forced into the spotlight simply by the presence of the man speaking from the Capitol.

Obama's inauguration was not merely a peaceful transfer of power. It marked the collision of two American narratives: the aspirational promise of "a more perfect union," and the defensive walls built to maintain white advantage. The moment cracked something open — joy and possibility for many, dread and resentment for others.

The history of America has always been a tug-of-war between progress and backlash. January 20, 2009, intensified that tension like a tightened rope ready to snap.

Hope took the podium that day. But resistance was already gathering.

Hope and Shock: The First Black President – Global Celebration, Local Disbelief

When Barack Obama took the oath of office in January 2009, the scene was unmistakably historic: more than a million people on the National Mall, television audiences around the world, and Black churches from Durham to Detroit treating inauguration week like a festival of deliverance. For many Black Americans, the moment carried a deep emotional weight — grandparents who had lived under segregation openly wept; young people who had never seen a Black president felt a new dignity in the public square. It was a symbolic rupture in a history that had long barred Black citizens from full belonging; this moment felt different and provided hope for better days to come for all Americans.

But the celebration was two-sided. In spaces where whiteness had long been equated with ownership of the nation, Obama's rise registered not as progress but as displacement. The shock many felt was rooted not in policy difference but in identity: a Black man in the White House became a visible, unignorable refutation of the old racial hierarchy. That dissonance — joy on one side, unease on the other — set the emotional frame for the backlash that followed.

White Political Identity Becomes Explicit: "Take Our Country Back" and the Tea Party

The rhetorical slider shifted from coded worry to an explicit rallying cry: "Take our country back." Where once political alerts were often expressed through policy critiques and elite channels, this phrase distilled a grievance into a mobilizing slogan that signaled loss of standing more than fiscal policy alone. The phrase carried racial freight: it was short, repeatable, and wide enough to unite economic conservatives, cultural traditionalists, and racial nativists under a single banner. Scholars and contemporaneous observers note that the Tea Party — broadly presented as a fiscal protest movement — rapidly acquired this racialized dimension as it grew into a major political force after 2009.

Public demonstrations, organizational materials, and the visual culture of protests often blended appeals over taxes and government spending with images and slogans that encoded cultural threat. For many participants—and especially for those receptive to racialized storytelling—the Tea Party was less a technical debate over policy than a populist revolt against a changing majority culture and a federal government perceived to be enabling that change. The political consequences were immediate: the movement supplied the energy that drove the Republican wave in 2010 and helped normalize a posture of reclaiming cultural control.

The Birth of Trumpism and the Birther Movement: Weaponizing a Name

The delegitimization campaign around Obama quickly moved from whispers to headlines. The birther movement — this false claim had suggested that Obama was not born in the United States — provided a simple, conspiratorial tool to question the legitimacy of the first Black president. While the rumor circulated among fringe actors early on, Donald Trump played a decisive role in amplifying and mainstreaming it by repeatedly promoting doubts about Obama's birthplace and demanding documentary proof; Trump's public embrace of birther claims made the conspiracy a household story and a political litmus test for those hostile to Obama's presidency.

That rhetorical strategy served multiple purposes: it painted Obama as an outsider, it gave political cover to those who refused to accept his authority, and it offered a culturally coded rationale—centered on heritage, name, and perceived belonging—to oppose his leadership. The deliberate use of Obama's full name in derisive contexts—"Barack Hussein Obama"—became part of this tactic, designed to evoke foreignness or divided loyalties and to erode the basic presumptions of American legitimacy. The tactic was not merely rhetorical; it was a delegitimizing strategy that primed audiences to hear policy disagreement as disloyalty.

Normalizing Racism in Mainstream Politics: From Dog Whistles to Bullhorns

A crucial transformation in this era was the shift from subtle coded appeals to overt public messaging—a movement scholars describe as from "dog-whistles" to "bullhorns." Where earlier political actors relied on implicit or symbolic signals to communicate racially charged messages, by the 2010s, those signals were increasingly spoken aloud and amplified by powerful media platforms. Research and analysis of political rhetoric in the period find a measurable trend: appeals that had once been carefully veiled became explicit and frequent, and the cultural norms that once policed blatant bigotry weakened.

In practical terms, this looked like several converging developments: memes and viral images that mocked or dehumanized Obama and other Black leaders circulated widely on social platforms; racist tropes and slurs migrated from the margins into mainstream talk-radio and cable commentary; and social media communities normalized patterns of harassment that had previously been taboo in respectable political discourse. The net effect was an erosion of the old norm: where once open racial contempt invited censure, astonishing to many, by the mid-2010s, it more often found amplification and organizing power.

These themes together show a clear pathway: a globally celebrated inauguration exposed deep domestic fault lines; those fault lines were quickly organized into political movements and slogans that carried racial meanings; conspiratorial delegitimization strategies were weaponized to question the First Black President's right to govern; and over time the channels of political communication normalized the very sorts of rhetoric that had once been relegated to the extremes.

Cultural Conflict Under Obama

The National Museum of African American History and Culture: Truth-Telling vs. the Demand for Silence

When the doors opened (September 24, 2016) to the National Museum of African American History and Culture on the Washington Mall, it stood not only as a building but as a long-delayed declaration: Black history is American history. Generations of stories once buried in basements, whispered in family rooms, or erased from textbooks suddenly stood in sunlight — enslavement and exploitation, resilience and brilliance, the horrors and the triumphs.

Millions celebrated. Elders walked through its halls as if through testimony — the proof of what they had always known. Yet that very fullness of truth provoked a predictable backlash. Some conservative voices labeled the museum "divisive," insisting that America should "move past" race, not display it. In this worldview, telling the truth about injustice becomes the real offense, not the injustice itself. Opponents did not object to museums dedicated to war victories or presidents; they objected to a museum dedicated to Black dignity, survival and resilience because truth threatens mythology. And mythology was the last defense of white innocence.

The Fight Over Confederate Symbols Intensifies

As a Black family lived in the White House, white supremacist ghosts demanded new attention. The Confederate flag — a banner raised in treason to preserve slavery — returned to the center of national dispute. Statues of generals who fought to keep Black people in chains were defended as "heritage." But the heritage being defended was the heritage of domination.

These monuments were never neutral. Many were erected decades after the Civil War — not to remember the past but to reassert white racial hierarchy and intimidation in the Jim Crow era. They were images of terrorization made of bronze, casting shadows over courthouses where Black people were denied justice and other strategic locations. Their defenders claimed patriotism while protecting symbols of rebellion against the United States — all to resist a future where Black citizenship was visible and powerful.

Obama's presence in the presidency exposed what the statues always meant. The "sacred" but sanitized story white America told itself — about honor, about "lost causes," about benevolent rule — cracked. In response, the backlash turned aggressive, as if history itself were slipping from their grasp.

Policy Battles Revealing Racial Lines

Obama's policy agenda — healthcare reform, policing reform, economic recovery — was not only contested but caricatured as an existential threat to America. To many Republican leaders, obstruction became a badge of honor, a symbolic barricade to protect "real America" from decline. It did not matter whether a policy helped the vulnerable — what mattered was staunch opposition and defeating the man proposing it.

"Law and order" returned as a rallying cry — not against crime itself, but against Black assertion. When Black communities protested unjust policing, the narrative quickly flipped: the oppressed became the problem. Dissent became disorder. Grief became criminality.

Say their names:

Trayvon Martin.
Eric Garner.
Michael Brown.
Tamir Rice.

Names that became movements — demanding equal protection under the law.

Instead of addressing the wounds exposed by their deaths, many leaders and media voices cast the protesters as threats. Armored police vehicles rolled down suburban streets, not into enemy territory but into Black neighborhoods and other places of protest. The message was unmistakable: state power would restore silence, not justice.

Criminalizing dissent served a political purpose — it reassured anxious white audiences that the old order still had teeth.

Obama's election did not create racism — it revealed what had been shallowly buried beneath political etiquette. The backlash was not merely policy disagreement. It was a struggle over identity, memory, and belonging. For every symbolic milestone that honored Black life, a reaction rose insisting that America must remain white in its bones, its heroes, and its story.

TONY L. SCOTT

Resurgence of Efforts to Silence Black History and Erase Trauma

In the years following the election of Barack Obama, a new front opened in the struggle over America's identity: not merely who votes, but who learns. The educational battlefield shifted to textbooks, state curriculum decisions, and public memory. Two dominant currents were at work: the demand to stop focusing on slavery and trauma, and the simultaneous push to maintain history in a form that preserves white innocence.

"Stop Focusing on Slavery — Celebrate America's Progress."

Across multiple state legislatures and school board meetings, criticism of curricula that included slavery, Jim Crow, and systemic racism grew louder. The new slogan: Let's teach America's success story — not wallow in its shame.

This rhetoric masked a profound choice: to omit the causes of racial inequality in order to preserve so-called social cohesion. Each time a classroom skipped Black accomplishment, each time a biography of Black achievement and excellence was removed from a reading list, the message was reinforced: We will remember what serves comfort, not what urges accountability, not what uplifts and emboldens Blacks.

Attempting to Erase Trauma and Triumph to Maintain White Innocence

The patterns of erasure trace back to colonization, but in this moment, they took new institutional forms. Museums were questioned, Confederate monuments protected, and history redefined. The trauma of chattel slavery and the triumphs of Black resilience were portrayed as unhelpful digressions from the "real story" of America: upward mobility, technological innovation, and global leadership. But removing those stories was not neutrality — it was revisionism in service of white power. *When history forgets injustice, injustice gets a future.* We are now living in this history.

Set-Up for MAGA's War on Teaching Racism

This cultural shift set the stage for the later assault under Donald Trump and his movement—the *Rise of Trumpism*. When white nationalists rallied around the idea that American classrooms were becoming indoctrination centers, a narrative took root: Teaching race = teaching guilt.

Under that logic, schools became spaces of cultural threat, teachers became enemies of heritage, and legislative efforts to ban certain histories or restrict educational content became a badge of patriotism. The war over teaching racism was the present manifestation of the war for power.

The Moral Compass of a Nation Fractured

It is clear to me that this nation, collectively — Blacks, Whites, and others — in overwhelming numbers—has lost its way regarding what I, as a child of God, call acceptable universal behavior, or the practice of once-overwhelming moral and decent societal or biblical norms that, in some measure, if not directly, provided guidance for this pluralistic society. America's moral compass is indeed broken. This brokenness is seen in every policy, practice, word and behavior that is antithetical to the moral teachings given in Scripture, by the God of the Judea-Christian Bible.

America's governing parties on both sides of the aisle are found guilty of gross moral failures.

Let me be clear, I am in no way suggesting that America or any other country is or should be deemed as a so-called Christian nation, nor that the teachings of the Bible should be used to legislate and govern a nation and its people.

That said, at the same time, a large number of progressives on the left and so-called revisionist Christians have embraced social changes — particularly within the LGBTQIA+ community — that many and even orthodox/traditional Christians view as contradictory to biblical teaching; I stand in this number. Those belonging to this community and their supporters are pushing or advancing pronoun designations, naming and gender recognition that, in my view, do not align with biblical truth or with nature's ordering, if you prefer.

Additionally, they were/are advocating for their lifestyle choices to be taught in schools and accepted or practiced wherever they saw fit. Books supporting their way of life could be found in school libraries and classrooms. This extreme shift in ideology gave conservative rhetoricians fresh ammunition. Among other policy decisions, not only did these conservatives rightly ban books that affirmed and taught the lifestyle choices of the LGBTQIA+ community, they also wrongly banned historical books that taught the truth about "America's first sin"—*Slavery*, and all that followed this horrible institution. Thus it was/is, under Trumpism, that those who opposed the Christian nationalist agenda were cast as cultural enemies. Bold, harsh language replaced negotiation; division replaced discourse.

Having once aligned with and voted for the Democratic ticket, and yet, I saw some of the good intentions of elected leaders from both parties. Yet the moral contradictions and flaws within both parties — and the extreme rhetoric of Trump and his loyalists — persuaded me to become an unaffiliated voter, subsequently vowing to vote no more. However, when this country's Constitutional norms and democratic institutions came noticeably under threat by Trump, as he sought a second term as president, I voted not as a Democrat but as one committed to the preservation of this nation's Constitutional ordering, its democratic norms and the Republic of America.

Today, under Trump's second term as president, those norms are in jeopardy and are subtly and systematically being dismantled under his strongman tactics. The Supreme Court and Republican representatives stacked in Trump's favor now stand at the forefront of efforts to undermine the democratic traditions they once swore and claimed to uphold.

America now stands at a crossroad and even a Constitutional crisis under the rule of Trump.

Christian Response

1. Remember Truth, Not Convenience

Christians do not shrink history to protect fragile identities. We testify to the full story — slavery and strength, oppression and overcoming — because the God of Scripture reveals truth that liberates. Erasing the past to preserve comfort is a betrayal of the gospel that demands repentance and reconciliation.

2. Hold to Moral Clarity Without Political Capture

Faith does not belong to a party. Christians reject both the cultural accommodation of the Left and the racialized nationalism of the Right. We judge all policies and leaders by Scripture alone — refusing to trade holiness for power or silence truth for political gain.

3. Stand for Justice When Institutions Fail

When government, courts, or churches protect the powerful and ignore the vulnerable, believers must become the voice that institutions refuse to be. God's people are called to defend the poor, confront abusive authority, and insist that righteousness be more than a slogan.

4. Speak the Kingdom, Not the Culture War

Christians are not disciples of grievance or tribal fear. Our allegiance is not to "winning" a nation but to advancing a kingdom that transcends flags and factions. We confront sin — personal and systemic — with the love, courage, and hope of Christ, refusing the bitterness consuming our age.

The Church must not mirror the fractures of society.
We are called to embody the alternative:

→ Truth instead of denial
→ Justice instead of advantage
→ Mercy instead of contempt
→ Christ instead of party or tribe

Our voice must remain prophetic, not partisan — rooted in the unchanging Word of God and driven by the gospel that makes all things new.

In the end, the Church's witness must be unmistakable: the cross trumps the confederate flag; the tomb defeats the ideology of domination; and every human being, irrespective of "race" or heritage, bears the image of God. May we walk in that truth boldly, repent where we have failed, and love as though the world's future rests in our hands — because the world's future rests in God's.

CHAPTER 10

A Nation at the Breaking Point: Race, Justice, and The Battle for America's Soul

The Blood That Reopened America's Wound

It began with a boy walking home with candy and iced tea.
Trayvon Martin. Seventeen. Unarmed. Targeted by a man who saw a threat instead of a child.
Killed after being followed, confronted, and judged guilty of existing in a hoodie.
And when his killer was acquitted, millions cried out the phrase that would soon define a generation: **Black Lives Matter!**

Not as a slogan — but as a plea.
As a warning.
As a lament.

Then came **Michael Brown**. Eighteen years old. Ferguson, Missouri.
Shot multiple times in broad daylight. His body left on the pavement beneath a burning sun for four long hours. A neighborhood watched,

children watched, the nation watched —a visual reminder that Black bodies too often become public crime scenes, but too often have not received public justice.

Eric Garner. New York City. Pushed to the concrete, arms pinned, a banned chokehold.
Eleven times, he gasped the words that still haunt America's conscience: *"I can't breathe."* The world heard him —but the system did not.

Tamir Rice. Twelve. Playing in a park with a toy gun. Police arrived and fired within seconds —a child killed before anyone bothered to ask his name. His innocence erased by the sight of black skin paired with a plastic gun.

These four names became a chorus — a protest litany — not because they were the only ones, but because each killing pulled the curtain back on the same truth: America was not post-racial. It was merely quieted for many Americans.

Other Names That Exposed the Wounds of America

Sandra Bland — arrested after a traffic stop and later found dead in her jail cell; a symbol of how Black women face state power.

Freddie Gray — spine shattered in the back of a police van; Baltimore erupted not out of chaos, but out of grief.

Walter Scott — shot in the back while running away; a bystander video proved what police reports denied.

Alton Sterling — pinned to the ground outside a convenience store and killed at point-blank range.

Philando Castile — shot during a traffic stop, livestreamed by his partner, a child watching in terror from the back seat.

Breonna Taylor — killed while sleeping in her own home; her name became a demand for accountability.

George Floyd — a knee on his neck for 9 minutes and 29 seconds; this time, the whole world saw — and believed what Black America had been saying for centuries.

Every story different.
Every outcome the same.
No justice! No Peace!

A Country Confronts Its Reflection

Each death struck a blow to the national myth —that racism had been solved by legislation

and washed away by time.

These tragedies did not create the crisis. They revealed it. They dragged hidden wounds into the open air where no one could look away and claim ignorance. White denial met Black testimony — and the contradictions were too large to reconcile quietly.

For many white Americans, the shock was in discovering that people of color were not shocked at all. For Black Americans, the amazement was in watching the world finally notice what they had been forced to endure all along. The message became unmistakable: A badge could become a license to kill — and a jury could become a shield for the killer.

Public grief transformed into public movement.

The marches, the hashtags, the kneeling in NFL stadiums, the raised fists on courthouse steps —this was not rebellion.
It was remembrance.
It was the resurrection of voices once silenced.
It was people refusing to let the dead die quietly.

From the pavement where **Michael Brown** fell,
from the sidewalk where **Eric Garner** gasped,
from the playground where **Tamir Rice** played — a movement rose.

Charleston: The Sanctuary Breached – June 17, 2015

The violence did not remain in the streets. It entered the sanctuary.

On a warm Wednesday night in Charleston, South Carolina, the doors of Mother Emanuel AME Church *(est. 1817)* — a historic fortress of Black faith and dignity — opened for Bible study. Members welcomed a young white stranger into their circle, prayed with him, read Scripture with him, and practiced Christian hospitality.

And then he murdered them! It was reported that this professed white supremacist was "hoping to start a race war because Blacks were taking over the country."

Nine saints — pastor, preacher, teachers, mothers, and intercessors — were gunned down in a deliberate act of racial terror. Their church had withstood slavery, the Civil War, Jim Crow, and the Civil Rights era, only to be pierced again by hatred seeking to incite terror by silencing Black lives as they sat before their Savior's feet, while in the service of their Lord.

This killer was not merely acting from personal wickedness; he was formed by a political climate of escalating racial hostility. The birther movement championed by Donald Trump declared Barack Obama an illegitimate president. Right-wing propaganda told white audiences their country was being stolen. Conspiracy and grievance became catechisms: "They are replacing us." "You are under attack." The shooter absorbed these lies, online and in public discourse, until he believed himself a soldier defending white survival.

Charleston exposed a sobering tension at the core of this nation: Black faith still gathers to pray, and white supremacy still enters with a gun, literally and symbolically.

Inclusion of Conflicted Symbols, Christian Nationalism, and Monument Politics

The massacre forced the country — briefly — to confront symbols long ignored. The Confederate battle flag, once defended as "heritage," flew high on the Statehouse grounds even as victims were laid to rest. Immediately following the attack, public outcry forced its removal — but by then the deeper question had been posed: what does a symbol of racial defiance cost a nation's moral conscience?

In the public debate that followed, defenders of the flag insisted it symbolized Southern pride and sacrifice; critics rightly insisted it embodied hate, oppression, and a refusal to reckon with genocide. This crisis of symbolism spread across the South and the nation.

Christian nationalism continues to play a key role in preserving these symbols. The idea of "a Christian America" means "a white Christian America," and the memorials, statues, and flags became sacred icons in a religious-political identity. The movement leveraged cultural nostalgia — God, family, country — to defend memorials of the Confederacy, recasting the "Lost Cause" as a spiritual war and thus honorable.

The names we must remember:

- *Rev. Clementa Pinckney* — pastor, state senator, voice for the poor
- *Sharonda Coleman-Singleton* — coach, minister, mother
- *Tywanza Sanders* — young peacemaker
- *Ethel Lance, Susie Jackson, Depayne Middleton-Doctor, Myra Thompson, Daniel Simmons Sr., Cynthia Hurd*

They were not simply "victims" — they were the true Christian Church of God. They were targeted because America has yet to repent and earnestly address its first sin—Slavery, and its enduring effects.

Charleston stands as a theological indictment: *If even prayer fails to grant safety to the Black body, then the sickness is not in the streets — it is in the nation's soul.*

This tragedy connected to the pain of Sanford, Ferguson, Staten Island, and Cleveland — but its setting, a Bible study, struck deeper. It revealed a reality: racial hatred does not merely challenge American democracy; it assaults the witness of the Black Church.

Charleston's grief spread into the bloodstream of the Republic:

A sanctuary became a symbol.
A church became a crime scene.
The cross and the noose stood side by side again.
And the nation could no longer pretend that the wound had healed.

The Rise of Modern Social Justice Movements

Grief across the nation turned into protest.

From church pulpits to city streets, from college campuses to online platforms, Americans demanded more than condolences—they demanded justice. What followed was not spontaneous. It was organized, patient, prophetic. And it marked the threshold of a movement that would challenge not just symbols, but structures and power itself.

A Look at Critical Race Theory and Intersectionality

From the late 1970s and 1980s onward, scholars such as Kimberlé Crenshaw, Derrick Bell and others developed a framework that challenged the idea that the end of segregation meant the end of racism. Known as Critical Race Theory (CRT), it argues that racial inequities persist because they are embedded in the very structures of law, policy, economy, education and social life.

CRT explained why, decades after the Civil Rights Movement, Black Americans continued to experience disparities in housing, schooling, employment, health and incarceration. It asked not just "who is racist?" but "what laws, rules, and institutions perpetuate the racial gap?"

To many American conservatives, however, CRT became a lightning rod. Suddenly, it was reframed as an attack on white children and white identity—portrayed as teaching guilt, dividing the classroom, and labeling entire groups as oppressors. The slogan "you are the oppressor" became a shorthand for what critics claimed CRT inflicted on young white students.

What began as academic inquiry turned into cultural warfare: CRT was weaponized in politics and education, and the discourse shifted from analytic scholarship to ideological battleground.

Intersectionality (1989) is a concept that grew out of CRT, expanding its analysis to include race, gender, and other identities' overlap in systems of oppression. In short, CRT is the broader framework; intersectionality is one of its offshoots. Unfortunately, these critical race frameworks and some of their activists associated with the LGBTQIA+ movement co-opted the moral authority and language of the Civil Rights Movement to advance their own cause—aligning their agenda and perceived "struggle" with the nation's historic fight for racial justice, even though the Civil Rights Movement was never conceived as a platform for issues of sexuality or gender identity.

The Social Justice Movement

Out of churches, campuses, community-organizing networks and conviction born of lived experience, a broader social justice movement emerged. It called for action beyond civil-rights law: confronting racism, poverty, mass incarceration, educational inequality and the legacy of systemic harm.

For many Black ministers, college professors, and grassroots organizers, this was a revival of sorts: the gospel of liberation in action, the "warrior zeal" of Isaiah applied to 21st-century America.

Yet the movement also generated tension, as some sectors accused it of being too radical, too adversarial, or too aligned with political activism; the movement was viewed as a threat to the white status quo. The question echoed: Can the Church or the academy hold both prophetic critique and evangelical hope? For those a part of these *just or biblical causes*, I will say the answer is, Yes, for the *true* and *righteous* Church of God.

The "Woke" Movement

Originally, "woke" meant moral alertness to injustice. It was a call from Black communities to watch, to awaken, to resist the unseen bias of everyday life. But over time, the word was also co-opted.

Many activists expanded the scope: "wokeness" also began to encompass gender ideology, LGBTQIA + rights, identity politics, and a broader critique of Western heritage. For some evangelicals and conservatives, this expansion became the straw that broke the cultural camel's back. The movement that began with racial justice was now cast as cultural revolution.

Where once the aim was justice, the critique became: the movement's agenda was shifting, broadening, and stirring pushback among those who believed their values were under assault.

Black Lives Matter: What We Believe

Launched in the wake of the unjust killings of Black Americans, Black Lives Matter Global Network Foundation (BLM) became a global moral witness. It affirmed: when Black lives are treated as less, we must cry "Black Lives Matter."

The movement rightly empowered local communities to demand accountability — from local police departments, from city governments, from national institutions. It shattered the myth that "racism died in the 1960s."

Pros: BLM put a spotlight on structural violence, motivated civic engagement among younger generations, and broadened the global conversation about race and justice.

Cons: Its founders also aligned themselves publicly with LGBTQIA + ideology, which alienated parts of the Black church, as well as conservative Black and white churches and communities. Many, including myself, perceived its narrative as attacking the traditional family structure rather than building it up. Organizational controversies — financial governance, leadership credibility — also gave critics ammunition to discredit and strongly oppose the movement's goals.

The following is the complete text of the Black Lives Matter Global Network Foundation's original 'What We Believe' statement, as it appeared on the organization's official website prior to its removal in 2020. It is included here for reference and historical context.

I have chosen to provide **bold print** where the language gives me pause and moral concern.

What We Believe - Est. 7/13/13, Founders Alicia Garza, Patrisse Khan-Cullors, and Opal Tometi

"Four years ago (7/13/13), what is now known as the Black Lives Matter Global Network began to organize. It started out as a chapter-based, member-led organization whose mission was to build local power and to intervene when violence was inflicted on Black communities by the state and vigilantes.

In the years since, we've committed to struggling together and to imagining and creating a world free of anti-Blackness, where every Black person has the social, economic, and political power to thrive.

Black Lives Matter began as a call to action in response to state-sanctioned violence and anti-Black racism. Our intention from the very beginning was to connect Black people from all over the world who have a shared desire for justice to act together in their communities. The impetus for that commitment was, and still is, the rampant and deliberate violence inflicted on us by the state.

Enraged by the death of Trayvon Martin and the subsequent acquittal of his killer, George Zimmerman, and inspired by the 31-day takeover of the Florida State Capitol by POWER U and the Dream Defenders, we took to the streets. A year later, we set out together on the Black Lives Matter

Freedom Ride to Ferguson, in search of justice for Mike Brown and all of those who have been torn apart by state-sanctioned violence and anti-Black racism. Forever changed, we returned home and began building the infrastructure for the Black Lives Matter Global Network, which, even in its infancy, has become a political home for many.

Ferguson helped to catalyze a movement to which we've all helped give life. Organizers who call this network home have ousted anti-Black politicians, won critical legislation to benefit Black lives, and changed the terms of the debate on Blackness around the world. Through movement and relationship building, we have also helped catalyze other movements and shifted culture with an eye toward the dangerous impacts of anti-Blackness.

These are the results of our collective efforts.

The Black Lives Matter Global Network is as powerful as it is because of our membership, our partners, our supporters, our staff, and you. Our continued commitment to liberation for all Black people means we are continuing the work of our ancestors and fighting for our collective freedom because it is our duty.

Every day, we recommit to healing ourselves and each other, and to co-creating alongside comrades, allies, and family a culture where each person feels seen, heard, and supported.

We acknowledge, respect, and celebrate differences and commonalities.

We work vigorously for freedom and justice for Black people and, by extension, all people.

We intentionally build and nurture a beloved community that is bonded together through a beautiful struggle that is restorative, not depleting.

We are unapologetically Black in our positioning. In affirming that Black Lives Matter, we need not qualify our position. To love and desire freedom and justice for ourselves is a prerequisite for wanting the same for others.

We see ourselves as part of the global Black family, and we are aware of the different ways we are impacted or privileged as Black people who exist in different parts of the world.

We are guided by the fact that all Black lives matter, regardless of actual or perceived sexual identity, gender identity, gender expression, economic status, ability, disability, religious beliefs or disbeliefs, immigration status, or location.

We make space for transgender brothers and sisters to participate and lead.

We are self-reflexive and do the work required **to dismantle cisgender privilege** and uplift Black trans folk, especially Black trans women who continue to be disproportionately impacted by trans-antagonistic violence.

We build a space that affirms Black women and is free from sexism, misogyny, and environments in which men are centered.

We practice empathy. We engage comrades with the intent to learn about and connect with their contexts.

We make our spaces family-friendly and enable parents to fully participate with their children. **We dismantle the patriarchal practice** that requires mothers to work "double shifts" so that they can mother in private even as they participate in public justice work.

We disrupt the Western-prescribed nuclear family structure requirement by supporting each other as extended families and "villages" that collectively care for one another, especially our children, to the degree that mothers, parents, and children are comfortable.

We foster a queer-affirming network. When we gather, we do so with the intention of **freeing ourselves from the tight grip of heteronormative thinking, or rather, the belief that all in the world are heterosexual (unless s/he or they disclose otherwise).**

We cultivate an intergenerational and communal network free from ageism. We believe that all people, regardless of age, show up with the capacity to lead and learn.

We embody and practice justice, liberation, and peace in our engagements with one another."

Conservative Perception

To many of the white evangelical, conservative, or some who are more aligned with the centrist population, these movements, real or perceived, took on a very different meaning: They were framed as anti-police, anti-Christian, or as a sort of Marxist revolution in disguise.

The fear: that the protest movements were not simply seeking justice, but power; that the identity of America as a predominantly white Christian nation was under threat; that the goal was not equality but reversal of roles.

This fear energized a backlash. What began as demands for reform evolved into counter-mobilization: political campaigns, grassroots organizing, social media campaigns — all shaped by the idea that the movements represented not only opposition to injustice but a threat, real or perceived, to heritage, religion, and national identity.

Conservative Perception: Framed as Anti-Police, Anti-Christian, Marxist Revolution

From the right-of-center media ecosystem and many conservative pulpits, the social movements that rose after the killings of **Trayvon Martin, Michael Brown, Eric Garner, Tamir Rice** and others were described in starkly hostile terms. Three dominant frames emerged and then circulated widely:

1. "Anti-Police."

- The phrase was shorthand for a larger charge: that movements like Black Lives Matter and sections of the social-justice coalition were not merely seeking reform of policing, but were actively hostile to law enforcement itself.

- Conservative commentators pointed to rhetoric calling for the defunding of police in some locales and amplified isolated calls for abolition as proof that the movement wanted to dismantle public safety.

- The frame worked because it converted calls for accountability into anxiety about rising crime and threatened personal security

— especially among white suburban and rural voters who view policing as central to order.

2. "Anti-Christian."

- Because parts of the progressive agenda (particularly on gender and sexual identity) conflicted with traditional evangelical and traditional or orthodox teachings, many conservative pastors and commentators portrayed the movements as hostile not only to public institutions but to Christian faith itself. However, many non-whites also held the same concerns.

- Symbolic moments (e.g., protests in church spaces, critiques of religiously inflected policies) were presented as evidence that activists wanted to supplant Christian norms with secular, even hostile, moral frameworks.

- This frame translated cultural change into spiritual warfare language, which made resistance a "religious duty" for many white evangelicals and a number of non-whites.

3. "Marxist Revolution."

- The label "Marxist" or "Marxist-inspired" became a convenient way to attach an ideological boogeyman to a wide range of demands (economic justice, police reform, racial reckoning).

- Opponents argued that the movements were not about humane reform but about redistributing power and upending American institutions.

- Once the "Marxist" diagnosis, whether legitimate or not, was applied to the Social Justice Movements, policy proposals became existential threats, not policy debates — a dynamic that tends to radicalize responses.

How These Frames Spread and Gained Potency

- Media amplification: Cable channels, talk radio, and conservative websites repeated and expanded these framings. Repetition made fringe claims sound mainstream.

- Social media virality: Short clips, worst-case examples, and sensational headlines spread faster than nuance. Viral content compressed complex debates into emotional flash points.

- Clergy and influencers: Pastors, authors, and religious leaders turned cultural objections into pastoral imperatives, framing political resistance as spiritual fidelity.

- Political actors and think tanks: Some political operatives and conservative think tanks supplied talking points, model legislation, and legal strategies to convert cultural fear into policy action (e.g., banning certain curricula, tightening speech codes in schools).

Consequences of the Conservative Framing

- Erosion of trust between communities and institutions (police, schools, local and Federal government).

- Lawmakers enacted or promoted legislation that limited protest, restricted classroom content, and punished perceived or real "indoctrination."

- A moral panic developed among conservative constituencies — especially white evangelicals — galvanizing turnout, fundraising, and the growth of paramilitary sentiment in certain circles.

Why These Movements Triggered a Different Kind of Backlash

The backlash against 21st-century social and or racial-justice movements was not simply political disagreement. It represented the collision of two deep, existential fears that, when fused, produced an especially combustible narrative.

Fear A — Exposing Racism Threatens White Innocence

- For many white Americans, the public exposure of systemic racism ruptured the story they had been told about national progress: that the law fixed injustice and time healed wounds.

- Admitting systemic culpability implied moral guilt and social responsibility. For some, that admission threatened social status, civic pride, and a psychological narrative of innocence.

- The rhetorical result: acknowledging racism came to feel like an accusation against entire communities — not just institutions.

Fear B — LGBTQIA+ Visibility Challenges Biblical Norms

- At the same time, expanded public acceptance and legal recognition of LGBTQIA+ rights touched a different nerve. For traditionalists, this was not a narrow policy debate but a challenge to a socially and theologically grounded moral order.

- Where social and or racial justice called for structural humility, gender and sexual-identity change demanded theological courage — for many conservatives and others, it signaled moral collapse.

The Fusion: "Trojan Horse" Narratives and Moral Panic

- These two fears fused into a single argument that circulated broadly among right-wing media and activists: racial justice = cultural revolution.

- The claim was that movements for race were a Trojan horse: hiding or downplaying an agenda that would remake family, school, and church. Thus, critics, like myself, argued, the movement was not merely against police brutality — it aimed to overturn the *moral foundations of society.*

- Once fused, the narrative justified extr͟
  public school curriculum bans, attacks͟
  vigorous "anti-woke" political ͟
  dehumanization of opponents.͟
  conservatives and white evang͟
  extremism or Trumpism.

How the Fusion Energized the Far Right and MAGA Movements

- Mobilization: The combined narrative turned defensive anxiety into proactive political energy. Voters were not only told to oppose single policies but to defend a threatened way of life.

- Militarization of Language: Political language hardened from "disagreement" to "defense;" metaphors of war, invasion, and replacement moved into mainstream conservative discourse.

- Sanctioning of Extreme Actors: As the moral stakes rose, fringe actors — militia groups, online extremists, some paramilitary collectives — found ideological cover. If the nation itself was at stake, extraordinary actions were framed as proportionate.

- Normalization of "Holy War" Rhetoric: For a subset of extremists, the combination of race and cultural grievances dangerously metamorphosed into a quasi-religious fight — not merely for political control but for so-called spiritual destiny. This empowered a minority to imagine violence as sanctified defense, with Trump being viewed as chosen by God and likened to their modern-day King Cyrus and liberator of the Bible.

Real-World Effects

- A spike in threats against school boards, teachers, and public officials implementing inclusive curricula.

- Legislative campaigns to restrict educational content, limit protest rights, and roll back civil-rights protections.

- Increased recruitment and visibility of extremist groups that present themselves as defenders of faith and nation.

- Deepened social polarization, making compromise and nuanced public conversation increasingly rare.

The conservative framing and the fusion of fears did not simply produce talking points; they produced a political environment in which every cultural shift could be read as an existential assault. What began as calls for accountability and fuller inclusion became, in the view of many conservatives, justification for defensive politics — the very politics that would later be mobilized into Trumpism or the broader MAGA coalition.

And so it is, as I draw my conclusion on the matters before us; in large part, the gains of the Civil Rights Era have come under staunch assault by Trump and his loyalists because the agenda of the LGBTQIA+ was associated with Black liberation and equality. If not in large part, certainly an accelerant for *The Rise of Trumpism.*

The Coming Storm – A Population Believing Violence May Be Necessary

When political rhetoric moves from argument to existential threat, societies begin to organize for confrontation. The racial storm intensifying in the 2010s and into the 2020s was not accidental; it was the product of accumulated grievance, a steady erosion of trust, and the amplification of a political voice willing to stoke fear and division rather than soothe it with a tone and language of calm and reconciliation. While failures and excesses have appeared across the political spectrum, the latter Trump presidency and Trump-aligned Republican leaders exponentially intensified a dangerous style of leadership—one that repeatedly embraced divisive, threatening language and challenges to democratic norms. That shift turned private resentment into public mobilization— hence, Trumpism.

Preparing for Civil War Becomes Public

What had once been murmurs in private chatrooms and fringe forums moved into public view. Conversations about training, stockpiling weaponry, etcetera, and defensive strategies that were once marginalized became normalized in open-air rallies and social media feeds. Paramilitary drills, tactical gear at pageant-like gatherings, and open talk of "defending our towns and nation" migrated from the margins to the mainstream. The logic was stark and simple: if public institutions could no longer be trusted to preserve an ordered way of life, then private citizens must take that preservation into their own hands. That idea—self-substitution for public authority has turned civil anxiety into preparations for armed defense.

This mobilization of whites is nothing new; however, it has grown and intensified in its resolve as defender of "their America." Some Blacks in countermeasures have begun to organize and arm themselves as they view the Trumpian coalition as an existential threat, solely because of the color of their skin.

Militias as "Defenders of the Constitution and Christian America"

Militias and paramilitary groups reframed their mission in sanctifying language. They called themselves patriots, Constitutional defenders, neighborhood protectors—and they layered that language with Christian rhetoric. Labels like "defend" and "restore" are treated as theological claims. This framing did two things: it fused civic and religious identities so that political opposition felt like sacrilege, and it cast ordinary public institutions—schools, polling places, courthouses—as potential battlefronts requiring paramilitary presence.

When political leaders and influencers echoed similar language—saying, in effect, that extraordinary times require extraordinary measures—the line between political rhetoric and incitement blurred. Trump-aligned leaders at times celebrated or failed to condemn these manifestations, lending them further legitimacy in the eyes of adherents. That tacit or explicit endorsement has made paramilitary posturing seem less like criminal fringe behavior and more like civic virtue to an expanding audience.

Social Fracture Deepens: Racial Resentment, Distrust, Demonization

In the 2010's the social fabric had begun to tear along old seams and new ones alike. Racial resentment began hardening into policy preferences and social suspicion; distrust of institutions hardened into a civic posture; and opponents have repeatedly—and increasingly—been portrayed as enemies rather than fellow citizens. The results were and has been immediate and corrosive:

- Racial resentment: Whites who had long felt dispossessed read every advancement in racial justice as personal loss; this fueled hostility and policy pushback.

- Distrust of institutions: Courts, legislatures, and law enforcement are increasingly read as partisan tools. When impartiality is doubted, private solutions replace public remedies.

- Demonization: Political opponents ceased to be merely wrong and became dangerous, un-American, or traitorous—language that has normalizes exclusion and, in extreme readings, violent preemption.

Reality: Two Threat Narratives, Two Survival Logics

As the crisis has deepened, two competing survival narratives hardened. One side believed and believes liberty was and is at stake.

For many aligned with MAGA politics, cultural change, legal rulings, and demographic trends were and are read as an existential threat to individual liberty and to an ordered public culture. Policies expanding rights or redefining norms became, and are currently framed as coercive impositions. This constituency saw and sees the defense of liberty as requiring assertive, sometimes extraordinary measures to preserve a way of life.

The other side believed and believes lives were and are at stake.

For Black communities and other marginalized groups, lived reality had long proven that "liberty" for some had meant continued precarity for others. Policing tactics, economic marginalization, and civic neglect endangered bodies and futures. For these Black and brown communities, survival required and requires accountability, structural reform, and protective measures—policies that often and do threaten the existing distribution of power.

Both logics are internally consistent—and tragically incompatible—because each views communal survival in zero-sum terms. The result is a political environment in which compromise feels like capitulation and concession feels like surrender.

Practical Consequences

The convergence of threatening rhetoric and organizational preparation has produced concrete, destabilizing moves:

- Escalation of rhetoric: Language of emergency and war has seeped into political speeches, commentary, and social feeds—normalizing images of battle and sacrifice.

- Paramilitarization of politics: Armed presence at civic events, school board hearings, and protests has become more common; for some, visible weaponry was intended to intimidate and silence.

- Erosion of civic norms: Traditions that had once tempered conflict—respecting electoral outcomes, adhering to judicial review, accepting peaceful transitions—are repeatedly tested and at times openly flouted by political actors seeking advantage.

- Increased threats and targeted violence: From plots against public officials to attacks on faith communities, the rhetoric feeds real acts of intimidation and violence that target both individuals and institutions.

Moral Weight

This is not merely a political failure; it is a moral crisis. When fear and grievance become organizing principles, the social imagination narrows to immediate survival tactics at the expense of long-term flourishing. The public square turns into a siege theater; trust erodes; and the slow, costly work of mutual recognition—of law, memory, and civic trust—becomes harder to repair. This is the current condition of America. As I see it, as well as those who are not Trump loyalists, America is at a moral crossroads.

Christian Response

We conclude this chapter not with a partisan clap but with a pastoral and godly summons. The stakes are moral and eternal; the choices are political and temporal. The Church must speak firmly and faithfully in a moment when the nation teeters toward violence.

Turn from Violence — The Gospel Rejects the Sword

Jesus taught his followers to turn the other cheek, to love enemies, and to bind wounds. The modern temptation to treat political contest as warfare is a Christ-denying distortion. The Church must repudiate any theology that sanctifies violence. No cause as presented on these pages requires taking life can be reconciled with the gospel.

Reclaim the Language of Patriotism for Love of Neighbor

Patriotism must be reframed. Loving one's country does not mean preserving privilege or silencing inconvenient truths. True patriotism in a Christian key loves neighbor — all neighbors — and seeks the common good. We must teach that defending the Constitution includes defending the rights of the vulnerable, not only the comfort of the powerful.

Defend Institutions, Reform Them When They Fail

The Church should both support the rule of law and demand its perfecting. When courts, police, or legislatures betray justice, faith communities must be prophetic: call out failure, demand reform, and press for accountability. This is not partisan allegiance; it is stewardship of the common life.

Resist Apocalyptic Narratives and Reject Scapegoating

Christians must refuse stories that reduce complex social questions into narratives of existential enemies. Scapegoating others as enemies of God or country is idolatry. Instead of stoking fear, the Church should model honest confession, repentance, and the slow work of reconciliation.

Practice Courageous, Nonviolent Solidarity

The gospel calls for costly solidarity with the oppressed. This means praying with, protesting alongside, and advocating for those whose lives are threatened — not as political props but as image-bearers of God. It also means offering pastoral care to those terrified by cultural change, helping them grieve loss without embracing hatred.

Lead in Rebuilding Civic Habits

The Church is uniquely positioned to rebuild civic trust through practices that cultivate character:

- Regular, humble confession where the Church has been complicit

- Acts of reparative justice — service, investment, partnerships — that rebuild relationships

- Forums for honest conversation that practice listening rather than victory

CHAPTER 11

The Trump Era
A New Era of White Supremacy, 2016-2020

Trump's Election and the Resurgence of Racism (2016)

The 2016 presidential contest marked an abrupt shift in American politics. Donald Trump ran a campaign that tapped into economic anxiety, cultural identity fears, and demographic change—but he also unleashed a surge of racially coded and, at times, overt rhetoric. Campaign slogans like "Make America Great Again" served not only as appeals to "forgotten" working-class Americans, but also as coded rebukes to a multiracial, multicultural America on the move. The campaign employed targeted advertising that sought to suppress Black turnout.

This election did not simply reflect underlying divisions—it accelerated them, elevating racial grievance from the margins to mainstream.

Normalization of Coded and Overt Racist Rhetoric in Political Discourse

Language once relegated to fringe forums began being uttered openly in presidential debates, rallies, and social-media streams. Terms like "illegal(s)," "they're coming for your jobs," and "you will be replaced" served as dog whistles and bullhorns. At the same time, established elites offered this discourse tacit endorsement by refusing to condemn it unequivocally. The 2016 campaign thus helped shift the Overton window: what was once extreme became acceptable. Headlines soon documented an uptick in hate incidents following Election Day.

In effect, the public arena lost its filter—racial animus found its voice.

Immediate Societal Implications and Concerns within Black and Minority Communities

For Black Americans, the Trump campaign—and subsequent victory—signaled symbolic regression. While not all voters embraced overt bigotry, the normalization of racial resentment sent a clear message: being non-white meant you weren't granted full moral consideration. Schools reported students making threats; Muslim and Latino communities reported increased harassment. The societal balance shifted. Where once Black Americans could hope the nation was progressing, they now confronted the reality: progress could be reversed. This concern was not abstract—it was grounded in data, lived experience, and amplified by social media.

For minorities, 2016 became an inflection point: the drift toward racial regression was no longer whispered—it was apparent.

Charlottesville and the Public Display of White Supremacy (2017)

The "Unite the Right" Rally: Participants, White Supremacists, and KKK Involvement

In August 2017, in Charlottesville, Virginia, hundreds of white-nationalist and white-supremacist marchers descended on Emancipation Park to oppose the removal of a Confederate statue. Participants included K KK affiliates, neo-Nazis, 'alt-right' activists, and white-identity extremists who explicitly chanted slogans like "You will not replace us." The rally depicted the convergence of open-hate ideology with public protest—unmistakable in imagery, flags, and torches.

Death of Heather Heyer and Violent Outcomes

On August 12, rally attendee James Alex Fields Jr. drove his car into counter-protesters, killing 32-year-old activist **Heather** and injuring dozens. The event was not simply a protest gone awry—it was a domestic-terror moment where ideology turned lethal.

Trump's "very fine people on both sides" Comment and National Reaction

President Trump's response triggered a firestorm. In his remarks, he said there were "very fine people on both sides," equating white supremacists and counter-protesters in moral standing. The backlash was swift and broad: hundreds of companies condemned the president, congresspeople called for censure, and the mainstream media framed it as a failure of leadership. Many whites, however, interpreted the remark as tacit absolution of their fears—and emboldenment of their cause.

Symbolic Message of this Event in U.S. Race Relations

Charlottesville revealed the profound truth that white supremacy had not faded away—it had been galvanized. It reframed the racial divide not as an issue of the past, but as a vivid present. Confederate symbolism became front-page news; torch-lit marches underlined that for many whites, the "heritage argument" masked a deeper struggle for identity. The rally's aftermath triggered nationwide removals of statues and monuments, yet it also galvanized white-identity networks, who described the enforcement of "heritage" as persecution. In short, the refusal to acknowledge and renounce the past became the battleground for the future.

These subsections set the tone for this chapter—charting how the Trump era fused electoral politics with racial empowerment for some, and acute concern and regression for others.

White Privilege, Immigration, and Policy Selectivity

The rhetoric of privilege resurfaced in the 2016-2020 era under Trump in stark and systemic ways. There was nothing subtle about it: when the then-president asked, "Why are we having all these people from 'shithole countries' come here?" — referring to Haiti, African nations and others — he uprooted any pretense of colorblindness in immigration policy.

This language is more than vulgarity; it is a signal. It told millions of people of color that they were coming from "undesirable" places, while immigrants from predominantly white countries like Norway or Ukraine — or South Africa under certain conditions — were framed as preferable. The policy decisions behind that language reinforced the racial import of immigration: selective admissions, protected statuses revoked, and a welcoming posture toward whiteness.

Globally, these developments sent a message: American policies were affirming a hierarchy of races. Countries with majority Black or brown populations were categorized as inferior or undesirable; countries with majority white populations were emphasized as ideal. This perception undermined U.S. claims to moral leadership and cast the nation's immigration conversation as one of racial preservation.

Moreover, this dynamic tied directly into deep historical fears of white displacement. Whites who felt unseen or economically squeezed found in immigration policy a scapegoat. The notion that "we are losing our country" became intellectually bridged by politicians to immigration reform. When white identity and status are threatened by demographic change, policy becomes the battleground — and immigration policy the weapon. In this era, the "privilege of whiteness" was being actively defended by law.

The result: Black and brown communities experienced not just exclusion but moral delegitimization. They were told their countries, their origins, and often their very worth, were under question. Immigration policy ceased to be merely economic or legal — it became racial theatre.

The Erasure of Black History in Education

As one front of the racial struggle shifted to policy, another front emerged in the classroom. In the Trump era, efforts to restrict teaching about Black History gathered steam. Some textbooks were revised, curricula challenged, and state legislatures pursued laws that limited how American history could speak of race.

These actions weren't isolated; they were linked to the broader "Make America Great Again" ideology. If the past is taught honestly — with the full weight of conquest, enslavement, and racial terror — then the narrative of a white-dominated America is destabilized. Reformers of this era thus invested in what we don't teach as much as what we do teach.

Ignoring or downplaying Black achievement and racial injustice becomes one way to preserve white comfort. Rather than acknowledging the full arc of America's racial journey, revisions often elevate a benign version of the past: one of upward mobility, benevolent institutions, and benign race relations. In effect, the teaching of Black history becomes optional, incidental, or ideological rather than integral.

For students in majority-Black schools, the subconscious message was that their ancestors' pain — and their own legacies — were optional in the curriculum. For white students, the message became subtler: that history no longer held racial reckoning, but instead offered national pride. The shift from "teaching discomfort" to "teaching heritage" is not benign. It is active erasure.

In this era, in some states and communities, education once again began to cease being only about facts — it became an ideological terrain where the future of racial identity, collective memory, and moral formation were contested.

If only the Truth of America's unfiltered version of History were a mandatory teaching in schools, I am convinced that its citizens, at least in large numbers, would reject any ideology of white supremacy. This would begin a concerted effort to dismantle systemic racism and create a more united nation. Because there are many who are in positions of power who are not informed about racism and its broader reach, this nation will continue to experience civil unrest by the oppressed and marginalized when injustice rears its ugly head.

George Floyd's Murder and the 2020 Global Protests

On May 25, 2020, the world watched as a white police officer knelt on the neck of a Black man named **George** for 9 minutes 29 seconds. The video went global. What followed was the largest wave of protests in U.S. history — and it wasn't confined to the U.S. more than 50 countries marched in solidarity, and media across continents broadcast the rupture of America's claim to moral leadership.

Under Trump's presidency, the federal response was combative rather than conciliatory. The White House threatened military intervention in cities, insisted "looting means shooting," and adopted an image of law-and-order over empathy. Domestic response soon collided with global narrative: nations that once deferred to the U.S. now issued scathing editorials denouncing American hypocrisy.

At the same time, the movement for reforming policing — for "defunding" or restructuring departments, for accountability, for saying the names of the dead — entered the mainstream. But the moment also revealed fault lines: to many conservatives, it looked like anti-police, anti-Christian agitation; to many older civil-rights advocates, it felt like the movement's radical flank. This duality showed that justice movements now operate in media-saturated, ideologically charged environments where racial trauma, generational hopes, and global scrutiny collide.

This was not only a turning point; it was a reckoning. A generation that believed racism had been overcome, confronted evidence to the contrary, and the world watched a country wrestling with its own soul.

The Intersection of Justice and "Woke" Politics

In the 2016–2020 era, the language of racial justice and the language of cultural change merged. On one side stood movements demanding accountability and transformation in policing, education, and economic life. On the other side stood a cultural backlash that read those demands as sweeping redefinitions of identity, family, and social order.

Re-examining Critical Race Theory, Social Justice, and Black Lives Matter

What began decades earlier in legal and academic theory found public and political expression during this period. Critical Race Theory opened the discussion: racism is not only individual prejudice, but embedded in law and social institutions. The social justice movement adopted that insight and pressed for systemic change beyond the Civil Rights era reforms.

Meanwhile, Black Lives Matter transformed Black mortality into moral urgency. Together, they sharpened the question: What kind of country do we live in—and who counts as a full citizen?

Renewed Call for Police Reform

The deaths of **Michael Brown, Eric Garner**, and **George Floyd** returned policing to the center of national debate. But unlike earlier civil-rights protests, these demands were fueled by video, by hashtags, by global witness—and by impatient generations who refused the slow pace of legislative change. Demands ranged from body-cams to defunding, to demilitarizing departments. For many white Americans, this sudden focus on the police felt radical, uncomfortable, threatening the institutions they counted on.

Tension Between Racial Justice Activism and Conservative Backlash

To conservative media and many white evangelical leaders, the rise of "woke" politics signaled more than reform. It signaled a shift in power—and thus a threat. Advocacy for racial equality was reframed as an assault on merit, heritage, and cultural legacy. Movements that once focused on ending segregation were now perceived as challenging traditional family structures, race relations, and even heterosexual norms. Critics argued that prioritizing identity and grievance over universalism created division, not unity.

Claims That Social Justice Moves Challenge Biblical Norms and Family Structures

For many, they believed, the pairing of racial-justice activism with gender-identity politics was combustible. When social justice platforms began endorsing Queer rights, inclusive curricula, and identity-affirming language, they collided with traditional Christian teachings. The result: many conservative whites and non-whites saw the "woke" movement and other social justice movements as undermining not only race relations but moral order.

Impact on Public Perception, Political Polarization, and Racial Discourse

By 2020, the conversation around race and justice was no longer simply a civil-rights debate—it was a national identity war. Polls revealed widening racial divides in views of policing and protest. Terms once reserved for extremist fringes—like "cultural Marxism," "white genocide," and "identity politics"—entered mainstream discussion. The result: a hyper-polarized public square where even calls for reform became filtered through partisanship, suspicion, and a racial lens. What had been moral urgency became, for many, a partisan cause. The thematic of "woke" versus "traditional" substituted for universal moral claim.

Christian Response

The Church stands at a fork in the road: will we become captive to ideology or freed by the gospel?

- We must preach justice—not just mercy—and stand without fear when the accused are our own.

- We must affirm biblical truths about family and identity without turning them into political logos.

- We must resist the temptation to reduce faith to a tribal badge. When Christian identity is co-opted by ideology—on either side—the gospel is betrayed.

- We must become agents of reconciliation, not warriors for one faction. That means not abandoning the homeless man beaten by police nor ignoring the worried father fearful for his community's safety.

- We must hold to the cross as the ultimate symbol of restoration—where division, not exclusion, reigns.

- Let our conversations be generous, our love courageous, our justice humble. In a time of polarization, faith must be the bridge-builder, not the divider.

CHAPTER 12

The Burden of Representation: Obama, Trump, Biden, and Harris in a Divided America (2008-2024)

Barack Obama – The Promise and the Peril of a Black Presidency (2008-2016)

The Symbol and the Shock

When Barack Obama was elected the 44th President, the world witnessed a moment that seemed almost inconceivable in the long memory of American history. A Black man, born of an African father and a white American mother, had ascended to the highest office in a nation once built upon the enslavement of his ancestors. To many, it felt as though the long arc of history had finally bent toward justice. Crowds wept, hands clasped in disbelief, while from Nairobi to Birmingham, from Atlanta to Paris, the image of Obama's victory was received as vindication for centuries of racial struggle.

I remember watching the television and seeing *Reverend Jesse Jackson* crying—a man who himself had once worn the mantle of a presidential candidate, who had carried the hopes of a generation that dared to dream of this very day. His tears carried the weight of that dream finally realized.

Like millions across the world, I too was glued to the television screen, watching history unfold in real time. I had my teenage son, Desmond, sit to witness this monumental occasion, a moment that many of our ancestors could never have imagined. The sight of Barack Obama being recognized as the first Black president—and the forty-fourth president of the United States—was fantastic. I felt the magnitude of what God had allowed us to see. Overcome by the significance of the moment, I recorded it on a VHS tape—a keepsake of history I still possess to this day. That night was not only a national milestone; it was a deeply personal and soulful affirmation that history, long written in blood and struggle, had possibly begun to turn a corner.

There were those—many among the older generations of African Americans—who had lived long enough to believe they would never see such a day. The thought of a Black man as president of the United States had been, for much of American history, an absurdity, a political impossibility. And yet, on that November night, the impossible stood before them in living color. In Obama's victory, the image of America itself seemed, momentarily, to shift—reshaped by hope, dignity, and the possibility of a redeemed national conscience.

But as previously mentioned, the jubilation of that moment was not universal. For many white Americans, the sight of a Black man occupying the Oval Office represented not progress, but tremendous loss. It unsettled a centuries-old assumption of racial hierarchy. Thus, Obama's election was not merely a political event; it was a symbolic reordering of power. It represented, to many, that could only be perceived as a "transfer of ownership." The White House, as its name unintentionally echoed, had been both a symbol and a sanctuary of white authority. To see that house now occupied by a Black family—by a man named Barack Hussein Obama—shattered the mythology of a white-ruled America.

The presidency itself became a racial totem, an emblem of belonging and exclusion. To some, it was proof that America's promise was still alive; to others, it was proof that "their" America was slipping away. And in that tension, the fragile unity that had briefly emerged in the glow of Obama's victory began almost immediately to unravel.

It was in this precise tension that what I call *The Obama Effect* and *The Rise of Trumpism* began to take root. The joy, pride, and global admiration that accompanied Obama's ascent triggered an equal and opposite reaction among those who viewed his presidency as a cultural and racial betrayal. The very symbolism of progress—embodied in Obama's grace, intellect, and measured diplomacy—became, to others, the spark of resentment and fear. This reactionary energy would, over the years to come, harden into what would later be known as Trumpism: a movement of grievance, nostalgia, and resistance to the racial and moral transformation Obama's presidency had come to represent.

Resistance in Real Time

The opposition to President Obama's administration began before his first day in office. Even as millions celebrated his inauguration, powerful undercurrents of resistance were already forming. Republican leaders quietly resolved to ensure that his presidency would fail—not through policy alone, but through paralysis. Political obstruction became a strategy of defiance. From judicial appointments to healthcare reform, every initiative he proposed was met with unified resistance, even when those same policies had once enjoyed bipartisan support.

But beneath the political opposition, there ran a deeper, unspoken current—the racial undertone that shaped the language and symbols of dissent. The chant to "take our country back," popularized during the early months of his presidency, carried meanings that were far more than partisan. It echoed an old and familiar fear: that Black authority meant white displacement.

The Confederate flags waved, and the chants rose not only in defense of fiscal conservatism but against the intangible unease of demographic change. While overt racism was often denied, the subtext was clear: the presidency of Obama had exposed how deeply whiteness remained central to the meaning of "real America."

Into this atmosphere, seizing upon the moment and opportunity, Donald J. Trump, a businessman whose opportunistic and Machiavellian instincts were keenly attuned to white grievance and suspicion. Trump, who financially supported either governing party and switched party affiliations as needed to benefit his selfish gains, understood what many politicians refused to acknowledge—that racial resentment, which he began to embody and express more openly over time, could be mobilized as political capital.

With calculated precision, he questioned not Obama's policies, but his legitimacy as an American. The so-called "birther" movement that Trump championed was not merely a conspiracy theory—it was a coded racial indictment. The birther campaign spread like wildfire, fueled by right-

THE OBAMA EFFECT

wing media and online forums that thrived on outrage. It was a direct assault on the very idea of a Black presidency. What began as a whisper of suspicion soon became a political chorus. Trump's persistence in questioning Obama's citizenship not only elevated his own public profile but also normalized racial conspiracy as legitimate political discourse. It became, in effect, the public reawakening of white grievance politics in the post-Civil Rights era.

Nevertheless, Obama, ever composed and diplomatic, refused to dignify the attacks with equal hostility. But the damage was done. The birther movement created a fracture in the national psyche—a permission structure for racial animus to re-enter public conversation under the banner of patriotism. It sowed the seeds of a new era in which truth itself could be bent to prejudice, and prejudice could masquerade as principle.

In this, Trump's rise in the field of politics was no accident. He was the mirror image of the resentment Obama's election had surfaced—the counterpoint to the hope that had filled Grant Park on election night. The era of "Yes, we can" was met with a resounding "No, you will not."

This was *The Obama Effect* and *The Rise of Trumpism* in full manifestation: one presidency unlocking the deep-seated anxieties of another America that could not reconcile equality with the world they imagined, nor progress with perceived loss.

Obama's presidency, therefore, stood not merely as a chapter of progress but as the beginning of a national reckoning. It revealed that beneath the veneer of post-racial triumph lay an unresolved question that America had carried since its founding: whether the full dignity of citizenship could ever truly belong to those once enslaved within its borders.

The Moral Paradox of Progress

In 2015, President Obama stood before a nation divided not by war or economics, but by morality itself. That summer, the Supreme Court of the United States legalized "same-sex marriage" nationwide—a landmark decision that reshaped the legal and cultural landscape of America. The ruling, Obergefell v. Hodges, was hailed by progressives as a defining step toward equality and inclusion. That night, in a symbolic gesture of celebration, the White House was illuminated in the colors of the rainbow flag.

To many, the glowing image of the People's House bathed in rainbow light was a triumph of liberty and love—an emblem of a modern, inclusive America finally extending its promise to all citizens. To others, however, it was a signal of moral decline, a public declaration that the nation had abandoned its biblical foundation. Many white evangelical Christians, Protestant Christians and others of varying faiths, who had once rejoiced in the symbolism of a Black president, now looked on in sorrow, believing that the moral compass of the nation had shifted from righteousness to rebellion.

And so it was, even among moderates, there was unease about the speed of cultural change—the sense that moral tradition was being overrun by modern ideology. For some, the redefinition of marriage struck not merely at policy, but at the sacred order of creation itself. What had been celebrated as progress in one America was mourned as apostasy in another.

This moment revealed the deeper paradox of Obama's presidency: the same leader who had embodied hope, reconciliation, and moral clarity for many had, in the eyes of others, become a symbol of cultural drift. His "evolution" and decision to align with the moral vision of inclusion marked a turning point in America's cultural war. What Obama and others called "evolution," others called "apostasy." I too was among the number of those deeply grieved by what had taken place. This was also a turning point for me, one who had been registered as a Democrat by heritage. Because of the moral failures I saw within both the Democrat and Republican parties, I became an unaffiliated voter, with intentions to never vote again.

The illumination of the White House in rainbow colors was more than a gesture; it was a sermon without words, preaching two opposing gospels at once—one of liberation, and the other of lament. The divide that followed was not just political; it was spiritual. It revealed that America's greatest fault line was not only race, but righteousness—the question of who defines what is right in the sight of God and country.

In that divide, *The Obama Effect* and *The Rise of Trumpism* gained new momentum. What had begun as a racial backlash now fused with moral resistance. For many white evangelicals and conservative Catholics, Trump's crude persona mattered less than his perceived willingness to defend the "Christian nation" against the tide of secular progressivism. Obama's moral vision had awakened their political militancy. His inclusivity, though noble in intent, deepened the chasm between progressive idealism and traditionalist America—a division that would come to define the nation's next political era.

The Afterglow and the Undercurrent

As Obama's second term drew to a close, the glow of his historic presidency began to fade into a more complex legacy. His calm demeanor, intellectual eloquence, and international respect were undeniable. Yet beneath the surface of that success, another current was quietly building—a current of resentment, disillusionment, and fear.

I think it's correct to say that Obama and his supporters' (I was in this number) idealism had underestimated the persistence of racial resentment. His vision of a post-racial America, where unity could be achieved through shared decency and dialogue, was sincere but premature. The election of a Black president did not end racism; it exposed it. It did not heal division; it revealed how deeply division was embedded in the nation's soul.

The illusion that post-racial America had been achieved masked a deeper white anxiety—a quiet dread among many that demographic change and multicultural inclusion were erasing the cultural dominance of the past. While the world celebrated the sophistication of Obama's leadership, millions of Americans felt unseen, unheard, and displaced within their own country.

His very success—his eloquence, his global stature, his scandal-free administration—became, paradoxically, the catalyst for backlash. For those longing for the return of a familiar order, Obama's presidency was proof that their America was slipping away. And so the search began, almost instinctively, for a political figure who could restore the old order—a man who would not apologize for the past, who would defy political correctness, and who would speak to white grievance without shame.

That search found its answer in Donald J. Trump.

Trump's rise was not the accident of political chaos—it was the reaction to the moral, racial, and cultural reordering set in motion by the Obama years. It was the shadow cast by the light of progress. Thus, as one presidency concluded, another America prepared to reassert itself.

And so the afterglow of hope and "Yes, we can" faded into the undercurrent of resentment. In that uneasy twilight, the stage was set for the full revelation of The Obama Effect and the Rise of Trumpism.

The Return of the Old Order: Trump and the Politics of Retaliation (2016-2020)

When Trump ascended to the presidency in January 2017, his victory was not merely political—it was cultural retaliation. *The Obama Effect* had stirred hope, broadened the moral imagination of what America might yet become. But beneath that hope, resentment had been ripening. The man who had once been the loudest voice questioning Barack Obama's legitimacy would soon occupy the very office he had spent years defaming. The irony was divine in its symmetry and tragic in its unfolding.

Trump's 2016 Electoral College victory—despite losing the popular vote by nearly three million—exposed the structural fractures within American democracy. Rural and exurban white voters, many feeling displaced by demographic and cultural shifts, found in Trump a vessel for reclamation. For them, his win symbolized the restoration of a social order they believed the Obama years had disrupted. It was not only about jobs, borders, or trade—it was about identity. And in this moment, the rise of

Trumpism became not an accident of politics, but a revelation of character.

For many of his followers, Trump represented payback—a cathartic backlash against eight years of a Black man in the White House. His campaign slogan, "Make America Great Again," was heard by many as a nostalgic call to order, but by just as many, a summons to restore racial hierarchy. The politics of retaliation had found its prophet, and he preached in rallies rather than temples, in tweets rather than policy papers.

The Anti-Obama Presidency

Trump governed as though his purpose was to erase the Obama legacy from the nation's memory. Every policy reversal carried the spirit of personal vendetta: the Affordable Care Act targeted, the Paris Climate Accord abandoned, the Iran nuclear deal scrapped. International agreements were not simply undone—they were publicly disavowed. Each repeal functioned like a declaration that America's previous moral compass had been defective.

But the opposition ran deeper than policy. It was symbolic, moral, and racial. Trump's America First doctrine stood in deliberate contrast to Obama's globalism. His rhetoric—infused with nationalism, suspicion of immigrants, and disdain for diplomacy—reversed the tone of American leadership. His frequent use of racialized or demeaning language—referring to "shithole countries," claiming "very fine people on both sides," and promoting the Muslim ban—reflected not just a policy stance but a moral inversion. It was as though each word was chosen to counteract the inclusiveness and dignity that characterized Obama's presidency.

The Obama Effect had briefly expanded America's sense of itself. Trump's presidency sought to contract it again—to pull the moral horizon back within the boundaries of grievance and nostalgia. It was not the dismantling of a policy framework; it was the dismantling of a worldview.

A Presidency of Polarization

From the beginning, Trump's war was waged not only against opponents but against truth itself. He declared the press "the enemy of the people," normalized conspiracy as common discourse, and introduced the term "alternative facts" into the national lexicon. Disinformation became the governing language of his administration. Lies were repeated so often that they took on the appearance of truth, and conspiracy theories were elevated to the level of national conversation.

This was not miscommunication—it was manipulation. Truth was no longer sacred; it was strategic. Outright lies were justified as "spin." Conspiracies were amplified through social media, where algorithms rewarded outrage over accuracy. The effect was devastating: millions of Americans came to inhabit a different reality, one curated by deception and shielded from correction. This was the post-truth era in full bloom, and it bore the mark of Trump's design.

His rallies became theatres of grievance—staged liturgies of resentment where dangerously divisive chants preceded prayers and loyalty eclipsed conscience. The revival of open racial rhetoric, unseen since the backlash of the 1960s, became both tolerated and televised. Through this spectacle, white grievance was not merely expressed; it was sanctified.

The media environment, already fragmented, became a battlefield of unreality. In Trump's America, to question him was to betray the nation, and to affirm him was to reject shame. Even moral vocabulary—words like "truth," "honor," and "justice"—lost their stabilizing meaning. Reality itself became partisan property.

Impeachments, Investigations, and the Absence of Accountability

Trump's presidency was shadowed by continuous investigations—into Russian interference, obstruction of justice, campaign misconduct, public scandal and later, abuse of power and incitement of insurrection. He was impeached twice by the House of Representatives: first for pressuring Ukraine to investigate a political rival, and later for his role in the January 6th attack on the U.S. Capitol. Yet in both instances, he escaped removal.

The trials revealed as much about the fragility of accountability as they did about Trump's transgressions. The Senate, bound by partisanship more than principle, refused to convict. The investigations that followed—from Mueller to Manhattan—exposed moral rot but failed to cleanse it. In the eyes of many Americans, justice bent beneath the weight of political convenience.

Those entrusted to uphold the law and preserve the Constitution often hesitated, rationalized, or retreated. The checks and balances that were meant to safeguard democracy faltered under the pressure of Trump's cult of personality. Accountability was replaced by avoidance, and moral courage by calculation. In this failure, Trumpism did not merely survive—it was vindicated.

Moral and National Crisis

Beneath the politics lay a spiritual unraveling. Populism, white evangelical nationalism, and resentment converged into a moral identity crisis. Trump did not create these forces—he harnessed them. His presidency exposed wounds left raw by slavery, civil rights resistance, and the racial backlash that had followed Obama's election. These wounds were not merely reopened; they were made part of the political economy.

The evangelical embrace of Trump, justified by appeals to divine sovereignty or pragmatic necessity, revealed a theological compromise—where character was sacrificed on the altar of perceived political victory. It was a *Faustian* bargain dressed in patriotic colors. The soul of a nation that had once debated what it believed now debated who it was.

By the time Trump left, or should I say was forced out of office after the overthrow of the Capitol Building, America had not healed but hardened. Its divisions were no longer about differing visions of progress but about differing realities altogether. The rise of Trumpism ensured that even in defeat, his presence would remain—his rallies continuing, his lawsuits multiplying, his influence hovering like a shadow over every political conversation.

As the nation turned toward the 2020 election, it was not turning a page so much as revisiting a wound. The COVID pandemic revealed both the fragility of governance and the fatigue of conscience. When Joe Biden took the oath of office in 2021, he inherited not only a virus-ridden nation but a spiritually exhausted one—its trust fractured, its moral vocabulary diminished, its unity strained beneath the lingering weight of the rise of Trumpism. The age of Trump had not ended; it had only paused. And into that pause stepped a president who promised restoration, decency, and empathy—a promise that would soon be tested in a weary and divided America.

Joe Biden – Continuity, Crisis, and the Politics of Fatigue (2021-2024)

Inherited Division

When Joseph R. Biden Jr. took the oath of office on January 20, 2021, the air in Washington carried both the residue of fear and the faint hope of healing. Just two weeks earlier, the nation had watched in disbelief as a violent mob stormed the U.S. Capitol, attempting to overturn the democratic transfer of power. The shock of January 6th lingered like smoke in the chambers of American conscience. Biden entered the presidency not upon a wave of triumph but through the wreckage of a country fractured by anger, disinformation, and exhaustion.

He inherited a nation in crisis: a deadly pandemic that had taken hundreds of thousands of lives, an economy staggering under lockdowns, and a moral fatigue that reached across political lines. His campaign promise to "restore the soul of America" carried a moral urgency, yet it also exposed the depth of national despair. Biden positioned himself as the antithesis of Donald Trump—a restorer of decency, empathy, and stability in a country desperate for calm. His quiet demeanor, shaped by personal suffering and loss, offered a tone of comfort to some and the reassurance of normalcy to others.

Yet the very qualities that made him appealing to moderates—his continuity with the Obama legacy, his empathy-driven leadership—made him a lightning rod for conservative hostility. To many on the right, Biden was not merely a political opponent but an extension of *The Obama Effect*, the embodiment of what they viewed as eight years of liberal overreach. His presidency, from its earliest days, carried the echo of the cultural backlash that had given birth to *The Rise of Trumpism*.

The Battle for the Nation's Soul

From the moment Biden entered office, he cast his mission in moral and restorative terms. "We must end this uncivil war," he declared in his inaugural address, invoking both Scripture and history to call Americans toward unity. But calls for unity, though noble in rhetoric, met a nation too fragmented to receive them. The January 6th insurrection had not only exposed political division—it had revealed a national and spiritual fracture.

His faith-centered appeals resonated with some, especially among older Americans longing for moral steadiness. Yet to others, such language rang hollow in a climate of distrust. The words "decency" and "empathy" had lost their common meaning in a country where even compassion was politicized.

Biden's presidency soon became a test of endurance rather than vision. His early months were consumed with crisis management: rolling out vaccines, stabilizing markets, and attempting to hold a weary nation together. But as global tensions flared—most notably with Vladimir Putin's invasion of Ukraine (2/14/22)—Biden's foreign policy experience was tested in real time. The war in Europe brought moral clarity but also economic strain, fueling inflation and renewing domestic frustrations. Putin's war and human rights violations in Ukraine continue as I write this book, with no sign of letting up, even though Trump, before the election of 2025, said that he would bring an end to this war. And now, nearly ten months in office and nothing has changed.

Returning to my previous point: pandemic fatigue deepened into political fatigue. Inflation rose. Immigration pressures persisted at the southern border. Each crisis fed the perception that America was trapped in a cycle of survival, unable to look forward. The promise of renewal was overshadowed by a constant state of repair.

And yet, beneath these crises ran the same undercurrent that had defined the past decade: *The Obama Effect* and *The Rise of Trumpism*. Biden's presidency, though distinct in tone, was in many ways a continuation of the same cultural and ideological struggle that had defined Obama's years—a tug-of-war between inclusion and preservation, empathy and grievance, progress and backlash.

The Difficulty of Governing a Disillusioned Electorate

The longer Biden remained in office, the more the limits of his leadership style became apparent. The America he sought to unite was no longer merely divided; it was disillusioned. Political discourse had grown transactional and tribal, faith in institutions had eroded, and the very meaning of truth seemed negotiable.

Progressives, many of whom had supported him reluctantly, criticized Biden for not being bold enough. They wanted sweeping reforms—on climate, policing, and economic justice—but were met with incremental steps. Conservatives, meanwhile, branded him as too liberal, a puppet of the progressive left, and the lingering shadow of Obama's moral vision. Biden stood in the crossfire of competing expectations, governing a nation where neither side felt fully represented.

As the months passed, his approval ratings declined, not due to scandal but due to exhaustion. Cultural polarization intensified as debates over "wokeness," education, and gender identity became daily battlegrounds in the media. The word "unity" faded from the national vocabulary, replaced by slogans of survival and self-preservation.

The nation seemed to be aging along with its president—fatigued, aching, and uncertain of its strength. And through it all, *The Rise of Trumpism* never disappeared; it simply adapted as Trump seized hold of the old Republican Party and shaped many of its leaders after his likeness, while others became his loyalists, with there being others who left the Republican Party or no longer supported Trump.

The Shadow of Trumpism

No matter what policies Biden enacted or how sincerely he sought reconciliation, the ghost of his predecessor loomed large. Donald Trump's rallies continued to draw thousands. His social media posts still shaped the news cycle. Lawsuits and investigations did little to diminish his following. Instead, they deepened his supporters' conviction that he was a champion for their cause.

Trump's continual presence ensured that Biden never governed in peace. The former president's influence persisted like an alternate government, holding millions of Americans in an ideological reality of their own—a political and Trumpian twilight zone. Two Americas coexisted: one nostalgic, longing for a return to the imagined order of the past; the other aspirational, struggling to believe that the nation could still move toward its "better angels."

The presidency of Joe Biden came to symbolize this tension between endurance and erosion. His term, marked by not-so-steady feet, hands and weary eyes, was less a turning point than a pause—a brief intermission before the next act—the reemergence of Trump, in America's long drama of division.

In retrospect, Biden's time in office revealed the full measure of *The Obama Effect* and *The Rise of Trumpism*. What began in 2008 as a moment of transcendent hope had, by 2024, become a test of endurance for the soul of a nation now uncertain of who it was—and where it was headed.

Kamala Harris: Breaking Barriers and Bearing Burdens (2021-2024)

When Vice President Kamala Devi Harris took the oath of office on January 20, 2021, history seemed to pause long enough to catch its breath. Standing beside President Joe Biden, she represented a convergence of firsts — the first woman, the first Black and South Asian American to hold the office of Vice President of the United States. To millions, she was more than a political figure; she, too, was the embodiment of generations of deferred dreams, the long-awaited proof that the glass ceilings of race and gender could finally be shattered. The image of her hand upon the Bible — a woman of color ascending to the second-highest office in the land — was heralded as a milestone in the American experiment.

Yet, from the moment she assumed office, the symbolic triumph of representation collided with the hard realities of race, gender, and power. The jubilation of her election quickly gave way to a torrent of racialized and gendered hostility. She was mocked by conservative commentators, belittled by opponents, and often reduced to caricature by partisan media. The same nation that once applauded the idea of progress struggled to accept the face of it.

As vice president, Harris carried the expectations of millions — particularly Black women, who saw in her ascent both vindication and vulnerability. But those expectations existed within a political structure that limited her visibility and influence. Her every public word was scrutinized, her silence interpreted as weakness, her confidence recast as arrogance. The burden of representation weighed heavily: she was expected to lead, yet restrained from being seen to lead.

Political Confinement and Public Critique

The responsibilities assigned to her seemed calibrated for political peril. She was tasked with addressing immigration reform and border security — two of the most divisive and intractable issues in modern American politics. The stage, one may argue, was already set for failure, and many critics were waiting for confirmation.

Within months, headlines began to mirror old tropes: "missing," "ineffective," "unprepared." The same coded narratives that had dogged women in power for generations resurfaced in fresh disguise. Her laughter was dissected, her tone analyzed, her competence doubted. Conservative media painted her as the embodiment of "wokeness," while progressives grew impatient for stronger leadership.

The result was a paradox: a historic figure trapped within the machinery of a system not ready to embrace her rise to prominence. The very visibility that once inspired hope became a mirror reflecting America's unresolved discomfort with powerful women of color.

The 2024 Bid for the Presidency

When Kamala Harris announced her bid for the presidency in 2024, the moment should have felt like destiny fulfilled. It was framed as a continuation of *The Obama Effect* — the renewal of progress through representation. But what followed revealed something darker about the American soul.

Her campaign was both historic and beleaguered. She faced relentless scrutiny and caricature — not merely for her policies, but for her identity. Conservative portrayals of Harris cast her as the epitome of liberal excess; even so, the high priestess of "woke politics," an emblem of everything they claimed to reject. But more revealing was the quiet resistance she faced from unexpected corners: skepticism among white moderates, indifference among young progressives, and hesitation among segments of Black men who doubted her authenticity or felt disconnected from her vision.

Those who once opposed a Black president now recoiled at the prospect of a Black woman occupying the Oval Office. Her candidacy became less about her platform and more about what America still refused to accept. The symbolism that once inspired unity now exposes fracture.

When she ultimately lost the election, it was not simply a political defeat — it was a reaffirmation of white America's enduring racial and patriarchal order. Her loss whispered the same painful truth that had shadowed every chapter of progress: that each step forward in representation provokes a counter-movement to reclaim the old order.

Continuity, Collapse, and the Lessons of Leadership

From Hope to Hostility: The Arc of Three Presidencies and a Counter-Revolution

The sequence of Obama, Trump, Biden, and Harris reads like a national parable. Barack Obama represented the faith that America could rise above its divisions — the audacity of hope. Donald Trump represented the backlash — the determination to restore dominance, to undo what the first Black president had symbolized. Joe Biden and Kamala Harris represented fatigue: the exhaustion of ideals strained beneath the weight of endless conflict, where unity was promised but not realized.

The Obama Effect and *The Rise of Trumpism* were not separate events but two movements in the same symphony — progress and backlash, hope and resentment, unity and division. Each presidency revealed what the other concealed: that moral progress, without moral renewal, cannot endure.

The Failure to Reconcile the Nation

Across these fifteen years, from 2008 to 2024, the thread of leadership repeatedly failed to close the moral distance between race, religion, and national identity. America remained a house divided — not merely by party, but by worldviews. The ideological war between multicultural inclusion and white grievance became the defining struggle of the era. Every political conversation, every election, every school board meeting seemed to orbit that central tension.

Religion, too, became politicized beyond recognition. For many conservatives, faith became a flag; for many progressives, morality became partisan. In both cases, the gospel of love was buried beneath the rhetoric of power. The church, often silent when truth was on trial, became a mirror of the nation's confusion.

The Prelude to Trump's Return

By 2024, disillusionment with progressive idealism and exhaustion with establishment politics created fertile soil for the evolution of Trumpism. The promise of renewal under Obama, the retaliation under Trump, the restoration under Biden, and the burden under Harris — all converged into a single, weary conclusion: America's racial wounds had not healed; they had hardened.

The myth of a "lost America" — once confined to Confederate nostalgia — was reborn, now clothed in the rhetoric of freedom, faith, and patriotism. It was no longer about preserving the South but about preserving a white and whitewashed identity: the belief that America was once pure and had been defiled by what liberals called progress.

And so, as Kamala Harris's campaign closed and the nation prepared to turn another page, the air grew thick with the sense of return. Trumpism had not vanished; it had been waiting — sharpened by grievance, emboldened by memory, and ready to reclaim what it believed was lost.

Thus ended one era and began another. From the jubilation of Obama's election to Trump's defiance and disregard for democratic norms, from Biden's weary restoration to Harris's burdened breakthrough, the moral arc of America seemed to bend not toward justice but toward reckoning. As the nation entered 2025, it stood again at a crossroads — haunted by its past, divided by its present, and uncertain of its future. The next chapter would reveal that the rise of Trumpism was not a passing storm, but a gathering, turbulent climate shaping the soul of a nation that still struggled to define what it means to be free as "one nation under God."

Christian Response

The rise and fall of political figures—Obama, Trump, Biden, and Harris—reminds the believer that no leader, no matter how historic or powerful, can heal a nation's moral wound. Scripture affirms, **"It is better to trust in the LORD than to put confidence in princes"** (Psalm 118:9). Politics may reveal the fractures within a people, but only the Gospel reconciles hearts divided by fear, pride, and hatred. The Church must resist the temptation to baptize political ideologies as moral truth. Whether clothed in progressive optimism or conservative nationalism, human systems remain bound by sin.

The Christian's duty is not to become an echo of partisan speech but to become *a voice of prophetic clarity*. When Trump's rhetoric of resentment inflamed division, the Church has been called to speak truth without compromise—declaring that lies and conspiracy theories are not strategies, but sins. When the promise of representation in Kamala Harris stirred hope, believers were reminded that representation without righteousness cannot redeem a nation. And when political fatigue numbed the conscience of America, the Church's call was to awaken spiritual discernment—to **"try the spirits whether they are of God"** (1 John 4:1).

In this polarized age, the believer must anchor hope not in the revival of a party or the rise of a leader, but in the reign of Christ, who alone unites justice with mercy and truth with grace. The Church must confront both systemic sin and personal sin—understanding that racism, corruption, and pride flow from the same fallen heart. As

Jesus declared, **"Out of the abundance of the heart the mouth speaketh"** (Matthew 12:34).

The moral task before the Church is twofold: *to expose the deception that dresses sin in the garments of patriotism, and to extend the invitation of reconciliation through Christ. America's sickness is not political first—it is spiritual.* The Gospel, therefore, must not be wielded as a political weapon but preached as the only cure for human estrangement and the sickness of sin.

In the era of Harris and Biden, when the fatigue of division led many to withdraw from moral conviction, it is the charge of the Church to stand as both conscience and comforter. Conscience—to name evil without fear; comforter—to proclaim that God's mercy is still available. For **"if my people, which are called by my name, shall humble themselves, and pray, and seek my face, and turn from their wicked ways; then will I hear from heaven, and will forgive their sin, and will heal their land"** (2 Chronicles 7:14).

Thus, the true Christian response is not to retreat into silence or rage, but to reassert that every presidency, every protest, every policy is subordinate to the Lordship of Christ. The Church must remember that the Kingdom of God does not rise or fall with electoral victories but stands eternal. And as believers bear witness in this age of distrust, their task is not to defend democracy as an idol, but to model righteousness as a testimony.

In the end, the cross—not the ballot box—is where the true restoration of a nation begins.

CHAPTER 13

The Trumpian Ascendancy: Race, Power, and The New American Order 2025 →

The Shock Before the Shift

Before the rise of Trumpism, before the fractured rhetoric and rallies, there was another moment when America's soul trembled — the morning of September 11, 2001. The fall of the Twin Towers and the thousands of lives taken on that fateful day were more than a national tragedy; it was a revelation of fear and fragility. For the first time in a generation, America felt vulnerable. The towers that had symbolized progress, commerce, and global dominance crumbled before the eyes of the world. And in their smoke and ash, a new era was born — an age where fear would become both policy and power.

The attacks became the moral justification for sweeping surveillance, preemptive wars, and the vilification of entire peoples. Muslims, Sikhs, and brown-skinned immigrants became the visible embodiments of invisible threats. Islam itself, real or imagined, was recast as an ideology of danger. Patriotism became suspicion's twin, and the defense of freedom became the pretext for curtailing it. Thus began America's long descent into a culture of fear — a fear baptized in the language of righteousness and homeland security.

What began as mourning soon became militarization. The "War on Terror" extended far beyond Afghanistan or Iraq; it reached into airports, classrooms, and communities. To be Muslim in America meant to live under watch, to be perpetually asked for proof of loyalty. In those years, the seeds of division were sown — not only between nations but within the American psyche itself. A new "us versus them" emerged, one that redefined citizenship, belonging, and faith.

And yet, beneath the smoke and sorrow, another story began to rise. From the rubble of 9/11 to the election of Barack Obama, America sought redemption — a momentary rebirth of conscience, a sense that perhaps the dream could live again. But the deep moral fracture that 9/11 exposed would not heal easily. It would simply change form, finding new expressions in race, religion, and politics.

The shadow cast by 9/11 never truly lifted. Its echo lingered through the corridors of power, shaping how America viewed itself and how it treated others. Out of fear came policies; out of policies came precedents; and out of precedents came a new moral order — one that elevated security above liberty and nationalism above neighborliness. The politics of fear matured into the politics of identity, and by the time the Obama era dawned, the lines of division had already been drawn deep into the soil of the republic.

So, when America celebrated the peaceful transfer of power from Bush to Obama, the world saw a symbol of renewal — a nation seemingly reborn in hope. But beneath that celebration, old wounds were only covered, not healed. The orderliness of that transfer concealed the unease within the American soul. The same fear that followed the falling towers would soon reappear in new forms — cultural backlash, racial resentment, and political extremism — preparing the ground for the rise of Trumpism and the unraveling of democratic trust.

Orderly Transference and the Shadow of the Abuse of Power

In every age of upheaval, nations seek symbols of peace to steady the heart. After the smoke of 9/11 had faded, the peaceful transfer of power — a hallmark of the American order — seemed to reassure the soul of the republic. Yet even that peace bore shadows, unseen but gathering.

Unlike the chaos that followed the election of 2020—the storming of the U.S. Capitol, *January 6th 2021*, the defiance of certification, and the insurrection that marked one of the darkest hours in American democracy—the transfer of power back to Donald J. Trump in January of 2025 appeared, at least outwardly, to be peaceful and orderly. The inauguration unfolded beneath a veneer of civility: flags fluttered, the oath was spoken, and the cameras captured what only appeared to be the restoration of normal democratic procedure.

Yet beneath that polished surface lay an eroding, a hollowing of the nation's institutions. The transfer of power may have been procedurally sound, but the soul of America was deeply fractured. The republic had obeyed the rituals of democracy while betraying its essence. The country's wounds leading up to 2025 had not remotely healed; they had simply been cauterized by exhaustion and fear; even so, minimized, disregarded and overlooked.

Trump's early actions as the 47th President exposed the deeper truth — this was not an era of healing, reconciliation, nor restoration of order, but a time of retribution cloaked in legality. Within days of taking office, he began targeting those who had once stood in his way: officials who had testified against him, journalists who had questioned him, and even former allies who refused to align with his renewed vision of loyalty. The purge was not executed through mobs or riots, but through memos, firings, and administrative reshuffling — quiet instruments of vengeance masked as policy reform.

The lesson was unmistakable: authoritarianism does not always arrive through chaos. Sometimes it cloaks itself in order. The danger lies not only in open rebellion, but in the quiet normalization of fear. Trump's first 100 days in office revealed how the machinery of democracy could be used to unmake itself — not by force, but by compliance. Institutions obeyed; consciences hesitated; and the rule of law became the rule of power.

The Return of Trump and the Deepening Division

Trump's re-election marked not merely a political comeback but the reassertion of a movement that had never disappeared. His return to power represented more of the same—but magnified and amplified. What began as populist defiance in 2016 had evolved into a fully organized ideology of domination, bound together by grievance and sanctified by nostalgia for a nation that once excluded most of its people.

The return of Trump deepened the racial and ideological divide across America. The thin line between patriotism and prejudice was erased. In cities and small towns alike, the symbols of grievance—confederate flags, nationalist slogans, and calls to "take back our country"—reemerged with new legitimacy. Extremist movements, long operating from the margins, now found themselves welcomed into the mainstream. What had once been whispered at rallies was now spoken from podiums of power.

One of Trump's earliest acts was the creation of the Department of Government Efficiency (DOGE)—a bureaucratic reorganization touted as an effort to eliminate waste and duplication. In reality, DOGE became a centralizing mechanism for political control, dismantling long-standing agencies under the pretext of fiscal responsibility. Programs that monitored civil rights enforcement, environmental justice, labor protections, and fair housing were either defunded or absorbed into DOGE, where partisan appointees now dictated policy.

Within days, an estimated 125,000 (many more to be added) federal workers lost their jobs, many of them from departments associated with social equity, education, or environmental oversight. Whole offices dedicated to housing discrimination, workplace safety, and community development were shuttered overnight. Trump hailed these firings as victories for efficiency, but their true consequence was ideological conformity—a silenced bureaucracy loyal to one man—Trump, rather than to the Constitution.

The Department of Justice (DOJ) also underwent a radical transformation. Under new leadership, the Civil Rights Division was effectively gutted. Cases involving police misconduct, racial discrimination, and voter suppression were dismissed or indefinitely delayed. The administration's emphasis on "law and order" replaced equal justice with selective enforcement. In the name of protecting America, it began policing dissent.

Additionally, Trump's actions have been viewed as favoritism toward his supporters or favors extended to people he likes, as he has offered over 100 separate pardons, nearly 30 commutations, with over 1,500 pardons given to those involved in the attempted overthrow of the government and peaceful transfer of power. What an abuse of power!

Trump's administration then moved swiftly to undo the legacy of prior executive protections, rescinding dozens of orders related to fair housing, educational equity, and voting access. Oversight boards were dissolved or transferred to DOGE for "review," a term that functioned as bureaucratic camouflage for elimination. The policies of previous decades, particularly those rooted in post–civil rights progress, were methodically dismantled.

This was not simply a rollback—it was a systemic unmaking of the democratic consensus built since the 1960s. Every policy reversal, every appointment, every budget cut worked to reshape government into a reflection of Trump's ideology: efficient in obedience, ruthless in implementation, and unapologetically aligned with white nationalist and white evangelical sentiment.

The Trumpian ascendancy thus represented a new phase in American governance — not a restoration of greatness, but a rebranding of control. It began fusing political nostalgia with Trump's authoritarian ambition, transforming democracy into a stage upon which power could be performed but no longer shared.

The Trumpian order had ascended, and beneath the fragile Republic is trembling!

Unmaking the Promises: Executive Power Rollbacks and the Rise of Trumpianism Redux

The return of Trump to the White House in 2025 was not simply the resumption of an earlier administration; it was the fulfillment of a deferred agenda, a continuation of what had been interrupted. The stage had been set during his first term; some of the players were the same, only more loyal, and the ambitions, once constrained by opposition, now roamed unchecked. The appearance of order gave way to the machinery of domination.

Trump's second term has centered on a calculated dismantling of the progressive policy framework established under both Democratic and moderate Republican administrations. By executive order, environmental protections were curtailed, workplace safety regulations weakened, and labor unions stripped of collective bargaining power. The administration's guiding philosophy was clear: deregulation not as economic policy, but as ideological purification — the cleansing of "liberal excess" from public life.

Environmental safeguards enacted to combat climate change were repealed within the first six months. National parklands and protected ecosystems were reopened for oil and gas drilling under the pretext of "energy independence." Labor departments were restructured to favor employers, not workers, eliminating safeguards for minimum wage, overtime pay, and workplace discrimination. What had once been built to balance profit with people was now repurposed to serve power and private wealth.

Perhaps the most visible and symbolically charged campaign of this era was the systematic dismantling of Diversity, Equity, and Inclusion (DEI) programs across the nation. Trump declared DEI "a cancer of the woke mind virus," framing it as a threat to meritocracy and national unity. By executive decree, all federal agencies were instructed to terminate DEI offices, rescind related training contracts, and prohibit the use of federal funds for "racial preference initiatives."

Universities followed suit under threat of losing federal grants. Corporate America, pressured by legislative reform and public intimidation, began scaling back internal equity programs. The result has been a cultural reversal: a return to a time when diversity was tolerated but not protected, and equity was discussed but not pursued. Trump's administration calls it "the restoration of neutrality." In truth, it is the reassertion of hierarchy.

The ideological architecture for this transformation drew heavily from the **Heritage Foundation's Project 2025** — a sprawling 900-page blueprint that reimagined the U.S. government as an extension of a nationalist, Christian conservative vision.

Project 2025, formally titled Mandate for Leadership: The Conservative Promise, served as both the intellectual foundation and the operational guide for Trump's restructuring of the state. It proposed the consolidation of executive power, the replacement of civil servants with loyal political appointees, and the centralization of decision-making authority directly under the president.

The Heritage Foundation's leadership — Kevin Roberts (President), Paul Dans (Project 2025 Director), and Russ Vought (former Director of the Office of Management and Budget) — were instrumental in shaping the administrative blueprint. Their objective was not reform, but realignment: to remake government in the image of ideological obedience. In their public statements, they framed Project 2025 as the "second American revolution," seeking to "restore biblical values, strengthen national sovereignty, and end the administrative state."

Under Trump's direction, those ideals took on a more menacing tone. Cabinet appointments became oaths of loyalty rather than tests of competence. The judiciary, already reshaped by his earlier term, was further stacked with seasoned appointees, however, whose primary qualification was allegiance to the new order that was taking shape under Trump. Legal scholars warned that the constitutional balance between the branches of government was collapsing into a personalist regime — one in which the separation of powers existed in name but not in practice.

To the Trump administration and its intellectual allies, this restructuring was the embodiment of efficiency. To historians, it was the echo of something far older and **sinister in nature**. The parallels with **Adolf Hitler's book Mein Kampf** were both rhetorical and structural.

Just as Hitler's manifesto laid the ideological foundation for the Nazi reordering of society, Project 2025 served as the philosophical codex for Trump's New American Order. In both, ideology preceded governance — the belief that racial and cultural hierarchy was not merely a social fact but a divine mandate.

Trump's America is becoming a reflection of that logic. *The nation is not being governed — it is being remade.* The executive branch is not functioning as an instrument of service but as a theater of supremacy, a stage where strength is virtue and dissent is betrayal or "treason."

And through it all, the language of patriotism provides cover for the language of power.

Cultural and Historical Erasure: Reclaiming the Lost America

Let's revisit and go deeper on this matter that is once again before you. Every empire that rises on the promise of restoration eventually turns its gaze upon history itself. After reshaping the mechanisms of government and consolidating executive power, Trump's administration has turned toward a more enduring conquest — the rewriting of the American story. The ideological blueprints of Project 2025 found their cultural expression not in policy alone, but in the deliberate reordering of the nation's collective memory.

Trump's push to reinstate Confederate markers and erase Black history programs was framed as an act of national renewal — a "restoration of patriotic education." Under the banner of "Reclaiming the Lost America," monuments once removed for their celebration of slavery and rebellion were quietly restored under new federal guidelines protecting "historical integrity." Statues of Confederate generals are beginning to reappear in public squares and military bases, while plaques were rededicated with inscriptions emphasizing "valor" rather than "treason."

Across the South — and spreading into the Midwest — new legislation required the teaching of "balanced perspectives" on slavery, Reconstruction, and the Civil Rights Movement. In practice, this balance meant equating oppression with order, painting enslavement as merely regrettable by a few but a necessary chapter in America's progress. The national memory is being sanitized, one textbook, one monument, one classroom at a time.

Textbooks, museums, and public school curricula came under new restrictions, driven by state-level mandates echoing the federal tone. History teachers were instructed to avoid "divisive concepts," while museum curators faced pressure to "depoliticize exhibits." The Smithsonian's African American History and Culture Museum became a flashpoint of controversy, with proposed oversight boards to "ensure ideological balance." Behind the language of "fairness" lurked the machinery of control.

The attack on Black historical scholarship and cultural representation was justified under the rhetorical banner of "fighting woke indoctrination." Prominent scholars, artists, and educators were accused of spreading "anti-American sentiment" for teaching the history of systemic racism. Funding for African American studies programs was slashed across major universities. Grants supporting community archives and oral history projects were openly defunded. A generation of students was being taught not what happened, but what was permitted to be remembered.

This movement became the cultural wing of Trumpism Redux — a campaign to overwrite America's complex racial narrative with one of sanitized nostalgia. The past was recast as glorious, the oppressor as misunderstood, and the oppressed as ungrateful. The rhetoric of patriotism masked a deeper purpose: to erase the moral scars of history, thereby absolving the nation of its ongoing guilt. It was not simply about controlling the present; it was about remaking the moral imagination of the future.

The symbolism of this erasure reached its most striking expression in the unauthorized demolition of the White House's historic East Wing and Grand Ballroom, repurposed under the guise of "modernizing the Executive Mansion." These spaces had once hosted civil rights leaders, global diplomats, and artists whose works reflected the diversity of the American story. This destruction was not merely architectural; it was ideological. It mirrored the demolition of democratic norms or tradition itself — a physical act that echoed the deeper dismantling of moral foundation and collective conscience.

Even as I write this section, this matter is unfolding in real time. The bulldozers that strip away marble and memory are the same forces that rewrite history and redefine truth. America's built environment, its monuments and museums, are being recast as battlegrounds of belief — where truth contends with myth, and history bows beneath ideology.

The Trumpian crusade to reclaim "the lost America" is not about recovering a forgotten greatness; it is about constructing a convenient past — one free from accountability, repentance, or reckoning. And so, as the stones of the old White House Wing fall, the nation stands as witness to a new kind of war: not fought on the fields of battle, but in the fragile spaces between memory and meaning.

Authoritarianism, Violence, and Political Suppression

As previously stated, language became a weapon in the Trump administration's arsenal: rallies, social media blasts, public addresses—all crafted to cultivate an atmosphere of menace, volatility, and obedience. Trump's rhetoric did not merely signal anger or discontent—it incited it.

By casting Black and brown communities, immigrants, and political opponents as threats to "our way of life," the presidency redefined dissent as sedition and protest as permission for retaliation.

The consequences were immediate and severe. A surge of threats, assaults, and politically motivated violence swept across the nation, many tied to extremist groups emboldened by the tone from the top. Members of Congress and state legislators reported credible death threats and swatting incidents. The assault on Paul Pelosi (husband of then–Speaker Nancy Pelosi) on October 28, 2022—when an intruder struck him with a hammer in his home—became a grim symbol of how political violence could reach into the sanctuary of private life.

In June 2025, that threat turned to lethal violence when Melissa Hortman, former Speaker of the Minnesota House of Representatives, and her husband Mark Hortman were fatally shot in their home in Brooklyn Park. Authorities charged Vance Boelter with stalking and murder. The same evening, Minnesota State Senator John Hoffman and his wife, Yvette, were shot and wounded in an attack that investigators believe was part of the same spree.

In another high-profile case, Charlie Kirk, the conservative activist and founder of Turning Point USA, was shot and killed while speaking at a Utah college event on September 10, 2025. The bullet struck him in the neck, fired from a rooftop approximately 200 yards away. Prosecutors charged Tyler Robinson, 22, with aggravated murder, calling the killing politically motivated.

Ironically, Kirk had been a fervent supporter of Trump and conservative causes. His killing underscored a grim truth: no political alignment provided immunity when political violence became normalized.

An assassination attempt on President Trump himself only intensified the fervor among his followers; the event became a mark of martyrdom, hardening their militancy. Political loyalty morphed into quasi-religious devotion, with followers interpreting every public threat or act of violence as proof of a broader conspiracy—and justification for escalation.

The ideological blueprint behind these developments found real-world testing in the use of executive power. Under the guidance of Project 2025 and the newly formed DOGE, federal troops were deployed into neighboring states under the stated rationale of "maintaining order." In practice, these deployments blurred the boundary between domestic policing and militarized occupation. Constitutional checks and balances—once a safeguard against centralized power—were openly challenged, while white Congressional leaders and the courts (Trump loyalists) either complied or remained silent.

Gerrymandering and the New Architecture of Power

Nowhere was this authoritarian strategy more visible than in the redrawing of electoral maps. In Texas, Republican leaders spearheaded a mid-decade redistricting initiative—passed in August 2025—that produced one of the most unprecedented and racially strategic gerrymanderings in modern history. The maps were engineered to dilute the political influence of Black, Latino, and progressive urban voters, securing long-term dominance for the Republican Party.

State-level power grabs, particularly in Texas, exemplify aggressive forms of radical gerrymandering and voter suppression targeting Black and Latino communities. Behind this strategy was a profound fear of political loss. As the midterm elections draw near, growing signs of Trump's unpopularity—driven by public fatigue, fractured loyalties within the Republican base, and mounting criticism from independent voters and others—sparked deep anxiety within the party. Many strategists foresaw a possible collapse of their fragile majority and the erosion of the political dominance they had worked to consolidate.

In anticipation of what they perceived as a coming electoral reckoning, the Republican leadership—particularly in states like Texas, Georgia, and Florida—moved aggressively to redraw congressional and legislative maps. The intent was clear: to secure control of the political landscape before voters could deliver judgment at the polls. This preemptive gerrymandering was not a reaction to defeat but a fortification against it—a deliberate recalibration of democracy to ensure that power, once gained, could not be easily relinquished.

This fear of decline became the unspoken engine of a broader movement—one that sought to preserve minority rule under the guise of political normalcy. Gerrymandering, voter restrictions, and judicial alignment became the threefold cord of a system built not on confidence in the electorate but, the reshaping of it.

The alignment between Trump loyalists in Congress and a Republican-stacked Supreme Court consolidates one-party dominance, with most dissent silenced through procedural or political coercion. Federal appointments, cabinet selections, and judicial nominations increasingly reflect loyalty to Trump rather than constitutional fidelity, cementing a system in which executive power overrides checks and balances. The cumulative effect of these maneuvers—weaponized rhetoric, domestic militarization, violence, gerrymandering, and judicial alignment—creates a precarious and highly polarized America, where democratic norms are tested daily and the lines between governance and authoritarianism blur.

In this environment, reality bent. The language of patriotism, "law and order," and "taking back our country" masked a deeper transformation: dissent was dangerous, memory was suspect, and belonging was conditional. The architecture of democracy yet remained standing, but visibly teetering; its spirit was under siege.

The American Crisis and the New Global Order

The United States finds itself in an unprecedented political impasse. As of October 31, 2025, the federal government shutdown has entered its 30th day, a stark reflection of the deadlock surrounding Trump's so-called Big Beautiful Bill. This sweeping legislative initiative proposes a massive restructuring of welfare, healthcare, and social assistance programs, threatening the livelihoods of millions across the nation. The shutdown not only highlights the volatility of executive authority under Trump but also underscores the fragility of democratic institutions in the face of partisan extremism.

Amid this turmoil, economic anxiety merges with moral exhaustion. Citizens grapple not only with financial uncertainty but with the weariness of a country repeatedly confronted by political conflict and cultural fracture. Public disillusionment grows as the machinery of government, intended to serve the people, becomes weaponized to reinforce loyalty, enforce ideological conformity, and consolidate power.

On the international stage, Trump's foreign policy reversals further destabilize a world already in flux. Abandoning long-standing commitments to NATO and pursuing alignment with authoritarian regimes, the administration reshapes America's global identity, weakening alliances built over decades. Western democratic norms face challenges as the United States, once a beacon of cooperative governance, signals that power and influence can be leveraged through unilateralism and strategic dominance.

From these shifts, a new world order begins to emerge. It is defined not by collaboration or mutual security but by nationalist ambition, hierarchical dominance, and racialized ideologies. The parallels to early twentieth-century Europe are striking; just as authoritarian movements once rose under the guise of restoring national pride, American exceptionalism now bends toward American authoritarianism, where grievances are weaponized and loyalty trumps principle.

Domestically, Christian nationalism rises in tandem with this authoritarian drift. Theology merges with tribalism, faith becomes a political litmus test, and divine sanction is claimed to justify dominance. In this climate, *The Obama effect*, once a symbol of moral hope and racial reconciliation, increasingly seems distant, eclipsed by the fully realized rise of Trumpism—a movement rooted in grievance, domination, and control, seeking not just political victory but the reshaping of national consciousness.

The result is a United States internally fractured and globally destabilized: a nation where power is centralized, dissent is penalized, and democracy contends with both overt and subtle forms of authoritarianism. Here, history reminds us that the past is never idle; it is alive in the present, shaping the possibilities—and the perils—of the future.

The Cause and The Continuum

The events of Trump's renewed presidency cannot be understood in isolation. They are the culmination of America's unresolved moral conflict, this long arc of history in which racial, political, and spiritual fractures have remained unhealed. The divides exposed during Obama's presidency—the racial tension, the partisan resentments, and the moral and spiritual disillusionment—have not faded. They have intensified and metastasized, shaping the landscape in which Trump's return operates.

Nothing happens in a vacuum. The past lives in the present, and the present actively shapes the moral horizon of the future. *The Obama effect*, once a symbol of hope, moral aspiration, and racial reconciliation, has, in part, triggered the backlash now embodied in the rise of Trumpism. This chapter, thus, stands as both a reckoning and a warning: what we witness in 2025 is not the birth of something entirely new but the return of something ancient—the logic of domination, the manipulation of language as power, and the systematic reshaping of society under the guise of legality, order, and legitimacy.

This reflection, *The Cause and The Continuum*, compels us to see clearly: these developments are not simply political maneuvers; they are moral phenomena, woven deeply into the history of the nation. They remind us that history, ideology, and faith are inseparable, and that America's current crisis is both a mirror of past failures and a warning for the uncertainty of a nation, even so, the world and what lies ahead.

Christian Response

As followers of Christ, we are called to perceive the world not merely as it appears, but as it truly is under God's sovereign oversight. The events outlined in this chapter reveal a nation grappling with the tension between justice and power, truth and deception, mercy and domination. Scripture reminds us in Proverbs 21:1 (ESV):

"The king's heart is a stream of water in the hand of the Lord; he turns it wherever he will."

No human authority, regardless of its power, is beyond God's sovereignty. The weaponization of language, the erasure of history, and the threats and violence witnessed under Trump's ascendancy are serious and destabilizing, but they remain subject to God's redemptive plan.

Christians are called to act as agents of truth and justice, resisting fear, intimidation, and racialized power. In Micah 6:8 (ESV):

"He has told you, O man, what is good; and what does the Lord require of you but to do justice, and to love kindness, and to walk humbly with your God?"

Walking in this mandate requires bearing witness to truth, advocating for the oppressed, and sustaining hope in God's ultimate justice. History is not neutral; it is a moral theater, and God's people are called to participate faithfully, speaking courageously, loving boldly, and laboring for justice that reflects His eternal kingdom.

CHAPTER 14

The Future of America: Racial Justice and Its Uncertainty

How Did We Get Here?

Expounding further on the opening pages of this book: The story of racial hierarchy in America is older than the nation itself. Its roots reach back to the fifteenth century, when papal bulls such as *Dum Diversus, Romanus Pontifex*, and *Inter Caetera* granted so-called Christian European explorers divine sanction to conquer lands and peoples deemed "heathen" or "uncivilized." The *Doctrine of Discovery* became Europe's moral license for colonization: baptism by conquest, blessing brutality as virtue.

When these colonial imperatives crossed the Atlantic, they evolved into a uniquely American theology of dominion: *"Manifest Destiny."* Papal blessings were replaced with patriotic language, but the underlying logic remained the same—some were born to rule, others to serve, and domination was ordained by divine and national authority. The moral foundation of racial hierarchy, therefore, was not scientific reasoning, nor political expedience—it was perverted theology, misappropriated to justify conquest, enslavement, and exclusion.

In the nineteenth century, the convergence of theology and pseudoscience gave new tools for rationalizing inequality. Charles Darwin's natural selection was twisted into Herbert Spencer's moral creed of "survival of the fittest." Competition became justification for domination; non-European peoples were portrayed as separate and inferior creations. Scientific racism and *polygenism* offered a veneer of reason to support the same logic that had long underwritten conquest.

The lie persisted: European supremacy was a product of biology and divine favor. The truth, however, was far grimmer—their "fitness" was forged not in virtue or intellect, but in brutality, advanced weaponry, and systematic violence. Empire had baptized sin as progress, masking moral transgression with the rhetoric of civilization.

From Discovery to Domination – The American Continuum

These ideological foundations did not vanish with independence. They were woven into the architecture of the American state. America became the "New Jerusalem" of conquest—a nation formed by violence, yet cloaked in covenantal rhetoric, sanctifying domination as divine or patriotic duty. The logic of conquest justified slavery; slavery begot Jim Crow; Jim Crow begot redlining, mass incarceration, and educational inequities. Each generation repurposed the same lie, using new institutions and new language, yet the underlying hierarchy persisted.

The papal bulls of the fifteenth century became the plantation fields of the American South. The plantation morphed into Jim Crow laws, codifying segregation and subjugation. Segregation morphed into redlining and educational inequity, while the social and economic machinery of the nation quietly enforced the same racial hierarchy. America's racial past is not a historical artifact; it is an active architecture that continues to shape the moral and political structures of the nation today.

Every corridor of conquest and compromise leads to the present moment. The past lives in the present, leaving us with a fundamental question: ***how did we get here? It is a journey not of isolated events, but of an unbroken continuum of ideology, institution, and action—a continuum that binds divine sanction, scientific pretense, and political practice into a single, enduring architecture of racial injustice.***

Understanding the roots and continuities of America's racial hierarchy is essential to grappling with its present and imagining its future. The theological, scientific, and institutional frameworks that legitimized oppression for centuries still echo in contemporary policies, politics, and social norms. To move forward, one must confront not just the consequences but the ideologies and moral compromises that allowed them to flourish. The question of the future of racial justice is inseparable from this continuum: until we dismantle the architecture of domination, progress remains tentative, and uncertainty remains the prevailing condition of the American experiment.

The Church at the Crossroads of History

At this hour in history, the work ahead demands both truth-telling and spiritual rebuilding. The American story cannot be redeemed without confronting the spiritual complicity that gave its injustices endurance. The "Church," which once blessed empire and later sanctified slavery's survival, now stands at a defining crossroads. Its silence in the face of systemic sin has too often been mistaken for neutrality. Yet silence in the presence of evil is never neutral — it is participation through passivity.

From the colonial pulpits that sanctified conquest to the antebellum sermons that defended bondage, the "white church" has frequently echoed the rhetoric of patriotism more than the voice of prophecy. Its message, baptized in nationalism, blurred the distinction between Christ's kingdom and Caesar's dominion. The moral cost of this confusion is written in centuries of blood and segregation. But the call of Christ has never changed: **"You cannot serve God and mammon."**

Still, within the body of Christ lies the only enduring power for transformation — repentance, confession, and rebirth. No government program, no legislative reform, and no executive order can heal what the human heart continues to harbor. The healing of nations begins in the sanctuary of the soul. If the Church will again, as in the days of her origin, take up its prophetic mantle, it can yet speak truth to power, proclaim liberty to the captive, and announce a kingdom not built on race or privilege, but on righteousness and peace.

The Church must reclaim that mantle. It must preach not nationalism but the kingdom of God, not racial superiority but spiritual equity. The cross remains the only altar upon which the idols of race and power can finally be broken.

Where Do We Go from Here?

Dr. King's timeless question still confronts the conscience of the nation: "Where do we go from here — chaos or community?" The answer will depend upon whether America renounces its myth of divine exception and racial election — the dangerous belief that God has chosen one people or one nation for dominion over others.

The future of racial justice will not be built by policy alone but by hearts reconciled to truth. A new vision of community must emerge, one rooted not in dominance but in discipleship, not in conquest but in compassion. True reconciliation requires more than reform — it requires rebirth—the indwelling Spirit, God Himself.

If the church does not lead, then the lie of supremacy will lead again. History has proven that nature abhors a moral vacuum; *when righteousness is silent, power becomes its own religion.* The arc of justice bends only when the people of God refuse to bow to the idols of race and power. America's reconstruction — moral, spiritual, and social — must begin not in the halls of Congress, but in the house of God.

Where does America go from here? The moment looks bleak. The uncertain history is unfolding and yet to be written. The normalcy and democratic norms that I lived through and raised my sons under are now upon shifting sand and a faltering foundation. My grandchildren and perhaps yours as well, have been birth into a world of sin and increasing godliness. A world that has turned its back on its **Righteous, Loving and Just God.**

I now leave you with these words, only in part, that I have shared with my sons and others: *"You must root yourself in the truth of the Bible, so that your children at an early age may come to know God for themselves."*

That said, God is Sovereign; He yet remains in full control. Those who belong to Him, as one with my Father, our hope is not found or founded upon that which is terrestrial, but rather upon that which is eternal.

Christian Response

The history of empire and race cannot end in despair if the Church will remember who she is. From the wilderness prophets of Israel to the blood-soaked cross of Calvary, God has always raised voices in seasons of moral collapse. What history calls decline, heaven often calls opportunity. When the nations stumble under the weight of their own pride, God calls His people to rebuild the ruins.

It begins with repentance — not the shallow regret that seeks relief without renewal, but the deep turning of heart and mind toward truth. The apostle Peter declared, **"Repent therefore, and be converted, that your sins may be blotted out, when the times of refreshing shall come from the presence of the Lord"** (Acts 3:19). America's redemption, if it is to come, will not flow from politics or personality, but from the Spirit's power working through a repentant people.

The myth of divine exception — that any nation holds a unique covenant with God apart from righteousness — must be shattered at the foot of the cross. For Scripture declares, **"Righteousness exalteth a nation: but sin is a reproach to any people"** (Proverbs 14:34). No nation, however great its wealth or weapons, can claim God's favor while despising His truth. America became the so-called "New Jerusalem" of conquest — a nation formed by violence yet cloaked in covenantal rhetoric. But God does not bless conquest; He blesses contrition. He resists the proud and gives grace to the humble.

Therefore, the church must rise again as the conscience of the culture, the prophetic voice crying in the wilderness of modern idolatry. It must no longer echo the divisions of the world but embody the reconciliation of the kingdom. The body of Christ cannot afford to be fragmented by race, class, or political allegiance; for the Lord Himself prayed, **"That they all may be one; as Thou, Father, art in Me, and I in Thee"** (John 17:21). Unity is not merely a moral ideal — it is the visible proof of divine truth.

To heal the wounds of history, the church—the true child of God, must lead with truth and walk with compassion. *Truth without compassion becomes condemnation; compassion without truth becomes compromise.* The gospel demands both. It is the only power that can confront sin without hatred and redeem sinners without surrendering holiness.

If we are to build again what sin has torn down, we must first allow the Holy Spirit to rebuild us — individually, relationally, nationally. For **"except the Lord build the house, they labour in vain that build it"** (Psalm 127:1). America's reconstruction must be righteous, or it will not stand.

Let the people of God therefore rise, not with the weapons of the world, but with the witness of the Word. Let pulpits thunder again with the truth of the kingdom. Let hearts bend again in repentance. And let faith be measured, not by privilege or pedigree, but by obedience to Christ.

> Only then will the church cease to be an echo of empire and become again the embassy of eternity — the only city set on a hill, whose light cannot be hidden.

Postscript

The Burden and the Hope

History does not end with the closing of a chapter — it continues in the lives of those who inherit its unfinished story. The moral crises we face today did not appear overnight, nor will they vanish through politics alone. They are the fruit of decisions made, truths ignored, and powers unchecked. As this book draws to a close, I write not merely as a chronicler of events but as a witness to a turning point in the American story — a time when the soul of a nation stands at the edge of remembrance and forgetting, repentance and rebellion.

I am not a historian by profession. However, I have given much time and attention to the study of history, for I have come to understand that nothing happens in a vacuum — there is always cause and effect. Unfortunately, the public school system I attended offered little more than a narrow view of American history. The exhaustive and interwoven story of America, which is also Black history, was not told in the depth or truth that it deserved.

As a young man, I wondered why such deep racial divisions persisted. Around the age of thirty, I began to study with greater intent, tracing the stories and systems that shaped our nation. To my astonishment, I discovered that the struggles, sorrows, and victories of the Civil Rights era — events that shaped the conscience of a nation — reached their most significant milestones during the years of my own birth, 1965.

That realization changed me. It stirred a deep desire to understand not only the historical facts but the moral and spiritual forces that made them possible. As it was for me — wanting to understand how we got here as a nation — I now want those who read this book to understand how we have arrived at this point in American history: the year 2025, under the leadership of Donald J. Trump, amid the deep uncertainty that surrounds the American experiment. The ideologies and policies that shape this moment did not appear suddenly; they are the bitter fruit of long-planted seeds — of myths sustained, injustices ignored, and powers sanctified in the name of God and nation.

I have written this book because I want people to be informed — truly informed — about the racial dynamics and divides in America, and about the origins from which they came. There is truth in the saying: history repeats itself when one does not know it. History tells us where we are going because it reminds us how we arrived where we are.

But there is another reason I have written this work. Under the current presidency of Donald Trump, with a Republican-controlled Congress and a Supreme Court aligned in political and ideological sympathy, it has become increasingly evident that the democratic norms of the United States — once regarded as sacred — are being steadily undermined. Before Trump's re-election, it was clear that the Constitution, which once provided balance and stability, was no longer held with the reverence of past generations. Under his leadership, the nation faces not merely political change, but a moral and constitutional crisis — a reordering of what it means to be governed and what it means to be free.

As the United States undergoes this unprecedented transformation — this emergence of a new world order — I write so that the generations who follow me might understand how this republic, though imperfect, once sought order through its democratic process, yet began to unravel through the collision of what I have called **The Obama Effect** and **The Rise of Trumpism.** This book is both witness and warning — a record of how nations fall, not necessarily from invasion, but from within.

I write for this generation, but also for my grandchildren and the generations to come. I want them to understand the world they have inherited — its struggles, its fractures, so that they might rise with faith, courage, clarity, understanding in both history and the eternal and Sovereign governance found in Christ alone.

Yet even as I have traced the brokenness of humanity and the sins of supremacy, I have come to see a deeper truth: that God wants us to see the world's wounds so that we might long for His kingdom. We cannot rely on the governance of this world to bring forth peace or some hoped-for utopia, for the kingdoms of men rise and fall. But the kingdom of God is eternal. It cannot be shaken!

It is not my intention to condemn anyone in these pages. My purpose is to speak the truth with boldness, as truth must be spoken. The biblical message — the very Word of God — is a word of not only confrontation, but also of forgiveness, reconciliation, and healing. It is an invitation to repent, to rebuild, and to rediscover the divine image in every human being.

Though this book focuses primarily on the struggles and challenges faced by African Americans, I recognize that there are many others — people of color, the poor, the displaced — who have also endured the wounds of discrimination and exclusion. Their stories, though not completely told here, resound within my heart.

This work has been for me — a child of God, and preacher of the Good News of Jesus Christ — both a burden and a calling. It has taken me through history's dark valleys and across its sacred peaks. Yet through it all, I have found that the light of truth and the love of God still shine. And as long as that light shines, hope remains.

May we, as a people, remember that our healing will not come from policy or power, but from repentance and renewal — from seeing one another not as rivals in history, but as reflections of eternity; the imagers of God.

**"For the kingdoms of this world are become the kingdoms of our Lord, and of His Christ;
and He shall reign for ever and ever."**
— Revelation 11:15

— Minister Tony L. Scott
Durham, North Carolina 2025

www.ingramcontent.com/pod-product-compliance
Lightning Source LLC
Chambersburg PA
CBHW050518100526
44581CB00001B/28